Spelling
Teacher's Guide

Carol Matchett

Schofield & Sims

Free downloads available from the Schofield & Sims website

A selection of free downloads are available from the **Spelling** page of the Schofield & Sims website (www.schofieldandsims.co.uk). These may be used to further enhance the effectiveness of **Schofield & Sims Spelling**. The downloads, which are kept updated as necessary to meet the requirements of the National Curriculum, add to the range of print materials supplied in the **Teacher's Guide** and **Teacher's Resource Book**. They include the following items:

- **National Curriculum correlation charts** show you exactly where each National Curriculum requirement for spelling is covered in the **Schofield & Sims Spelling** pupil books. Page numbers are provided for reference to the relevant activities. Where appropriate, notes from the non-statutory rules and guidelines are included.

- **Supplementary spelling logs** reinforce the words from the statutory word lists in the National Curriculum. Accompanied by a brief **User's guide**, the lists reflect the order in which the words are introduced in the **Schofield & Sims Spelling** books and can be used to encourage pupils to monitor their own spelling of these words – for example, using one list each half term.

- **Tricky words extra** (for Years 1 and 2) lists examples of common words that are exceptions in some accents but not others.

- A further **My tricky words** sheet enables you and your pupils to make tricky words lists of your own.

- An **Alternative spellings** document gives examples of words that have more than one correct spelling.

Please note: Throughout the **Spelling** series, sounds are shown in inverted commas and spellings in bold: for example, the 'oi' sound and the **oy** spelling.

First published in 2013
Second impression 2014

Copyright © Schofield & Sims Limited 2013

Author: **Carol Matchett**

Carol Matchett has asserted her moral right under the Copyright, Designs and Patents Act, 1988, to be identified as the author of this work.

British Library Catalogue in Publication Data:

A catalogue record for this book is available from the British Library.

Commissioned by **Carolyn Richardson Publishing Services** (www.publiserve.co.uk)
Design by **Oxford Designers & Illustrators**

Printed in the UK by **Page Bros (Norwich) Limited**

ISBN 978 07217 1218 5

Contents

1 Introduction

Learning to spell

It is important that pupils learn to spell so that they can write down their ideas fluently and confidently.

Some pupils seem to absorb the correct spelling of words, with no apparent effort, during the course of their reading. The majority, however, need to invest more time and practice in learning to spell. Although there are certain tricky words with spellings that just have to be committed to memory, learning to spell is not purely about learning lists of words. It is about learning strategies, patterns, rules and guidelines that apply to whole groups of words – and applying these to make sensible and reasoned spelling choices.

Systematically teaching these strategies, rules and guidelines, while also encouraging pupils to monitor their own spelling, are key factors in helping pupils to become confident spellers.

Schofield & Sims Spelling

The **Schofield & Sims Spelling** programme is a structured whole-school scheme designed to develop pupils' spelling skills and knowledge systematically and progressively. The programme consists of:

● six **pupil books** containing activities that will help pupils to practise and learn spelling so they become accurate and confident spellers

● a **Teacher's Resource Book**, which provides photocopiable material to support the teaching, learning and assessment of spelling

● this **Teacher's Guide**, which helps you, the teacher, to plan, teach and assess spelling. Detailed teaching notes provide practical suggestions for how to introduce each page of the pupil books.

 Six pupil books

Teacher's Guide: teaching notes for all six pupil books

Teacher's Resource Book:
● extension and revision copymasters
● assessment resources

Schofield & Sims Spelling is designed primarily for pupils in Years 1 to 6. It introduces rules, guidelines and conventions and encourages pupils to develop the skills and strategies they need to become confident spellers who can monitor and correct their own spelling.

The programme builds on the earlier work that your pupils have completed using any systematic phonics programme. Book 1 assumes a basic understanding of letter–sound relationships and is suitable for pupils who have completed Phases 3 and 4 of the systematic phonic resource *Letters and Sounds* (© Crown copyright 2007) or the equivalent in another phonics scheme.

Pupils are taught that good spellers need to use their phonic knowledge – that is, the relationship between sounds and letters – in order to spell words. However, they also need to know guidelines, patterns and rules and to understand word structure and the relationship between words of shared origin. In addition, it is useful to teach pupils that some tricky words just have to be learnt, and to provide them with strategies that will help them to learn these spellings.

Schofield & Sims Spelling provides resources that will help you to teach and assess spelling. It helps pupils to practise and then consolidate and apply spellings, and can be used in conjunction with other materials that support this.

The programme is rooted in the following teaching model, which is explained in full in the next section of this book.

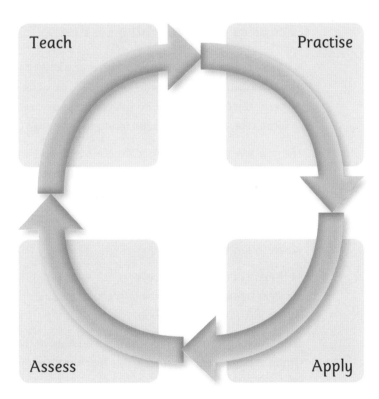

Teach — Practise — Apply — Assess

2 Implementing the teaching model

Stage one: Teach

Spelling is taught, not caught.

Schofield & Sims Spelling supports the systematic and explicit teaching of strategies, rules, guidelines and patterns to help pupils throughout your school to make good progress in spelling. Each page in the pupil books has a clear spelling focus and this should be introduced in a short and direct teaching session, lasting about 10 minutes. The teaching session may be carried out with the whole class or with a smaller group, as appropriate.

Guidance on how to introduce each spelling focus is given in the section headed 'Teaching notes' (see pages 27 to 80). These notes are designed specifically to help you teach spelling. They do so by:

● explaining how you might best introduce the focus

● clarifying patterns, rules, strategies or guidelines to be explained

● suggesting ways to model, demonstrate, explain or explore the guideline, pattern or rule in order to develop pupils' understanding.

Features of the teaching session

A typical teaching session starts with a quick 'Write and show' activity in which pupils are given words to write on a mini-whiteboard or sheet of paper. They then hold these up to be checked. Checking, comparing spellings and discussion of these 'Write and show' words helps to recap relevant prior learning ready to introduce the new focus.

The new teaching point is then explained, demonstrated or modelled. Spelling is a thinking process, so it is important to talk this through carefully, explaining the reasons behind each spelling decision and modelling the process of being a good speller. Pupils should be involved in making the decisions about how to spell and in writing the words. The key points for you to explain, model or demonstrate are clarified in the notes provided. You don't need to be an expert to teach these sessions.

At the end of the teaching session, the main points should be reiterated to ensure that pupils are clear about the key guideline, rule, strategy or pattern before they move on to practising it independently in the pupil book.

The 'Teaching notes' provide the page number in the relevant pupil book and also a reference to any copymasters supplied in the **Teacher's Resource Book** that can be used for extending or reinforcing the focus.

Stage two: Practise

Practice makes perfect.

In order to become confident spellers, pupils need opportunities to practise using rules, guidelines and strategies to help them spell words. The **Spelling** pupil books provide pupils with plenty of practice, giving them opportunities to develop their understanding of the focus introduced in the teaching session and to learn to spell appropriate words.

The pupil books are designed for independent work, with pupils working alone, in pairs or in a small group (see 'Working with a partner', page 12). There are usually two activities on each page so, if you are confident that the main learning point has been grasped, you might set the second as homework. A sample page from a pupil book is provided on page 8. It shows the main format and structure shared by all the pupil books and points out some of the key features of **Schofield & Sims Spelling**.

Answers are included at the back of each pupil book and pupils are encouraged to check their own work against the answers once a page is completed. This is designed to encourage pupils to monitor their own spelling and learning. Incorrect spellings should be corrected and learnt before pupils move on to testing each other. If you are worried that pupils might look at the answers before the page is completed, the answer pages can be fixed with paper clips and group or table monitors given responsibility for ensuring that they are removed only once the activities have been completed. However, it is always better to practise writing the correct spelling rather than an incorrect one, so it is not necessarily a bad thing if pupils occasionally check the spelling of a word they are unsure of.

It is expected that pupils will learn to spell *at least* those words included in the activities in the pupil book. However, many pupils will learn to spell more words than those listed because they will apply the general principles to new words.

As each page of the pupil book is completed, it will become an ongoing record of progress for you and your pupils. It will also become a useful reference tool for pupils to use when they are writing independently.

Additional practice activities

Some pupils may need further practice and reinforcement, while others will need extension activities. For this reason additional activities are provided in the form of copymasters, to be found in the **Teacher's Resource Book**. A reference to relevant additional activities is given in the 'Teaching notes'. Typical resources include:

● additional word lists, containing more words illustrating the same pattern or guideline

● word sort and word collection activities

● spelling logs, for selecting and recording words to practise.

See 'Supporting teaching and learning', pages 16 to 18, for further details about these activities.

The key learning point for the page is introduced.

An example is provided.

Words ending **ture** and **sure**

Remember

A 'chuh' sound at the end of a word is often spelt ture.   fixture

A 'zhuh' sound at the end of a word is spelt sure.   closure

Try it

1   All these words end with a 'chuh' sound. Read the clue and write in the missing syllables.

a) adv_____t_____ (an exciting quest)

b) m_____t_____ (a bit of this and a bit of that)

c) f_____n_____t_____ (tables and chairs)

d) p_____t_____ (you draw this)

e) c_____t_____ (to catch someone)

f) t_____t_____ (the feel of something)

g) fut_____ (not the past)

h) l_____t_____ (a serious talk)

2   Choose the correct ending. Complete the words using **ture** or **sure**.

a) crea_____   d) fea_____   g) trea_____   j) na_____

b) plea_____   e) mois_____   h) frac_____   k) struc_____

c) mea_____   f) lei_____   i) punc_____   l) sculp_____

Read–cover–write

Read this sentence and remember it. Then cover it and write it underneath.

Measure the mixture as shown in the picture.

_____

Check your spellings with the answers on page 46. Test yourself, or get a friend to test you.

I can spell all the words on this page. ☐   I can spell words ending with **ture** and **sure**. ☐

36

Pupils practise spelling words using the pattern, strategy, rule or guideline given above.

Target words and words introduced previously are practised within the context of a sentence. This encourages pupils to apply to their writing the point they have just learnt.

Additional activities further develop pupils' understanding.

This encourages self-checking, self-correction and self-assessment, so that pupils learn to monitor their own spelling.

The first 'I can' statement encourages self-assessment and review of the main learning points.

The second statement (in Spelling 3 to 6 only) reminds pupils to apply the learning focus to words that do not appear on the page and to their own free writing. Pupils tick this box when they have fully achieved the target and have used it in their own independent writing.

Stage three: Apply

Spelling knowledge is only truly learnt when pupils apply it in their own writing.

Perhaps the biggest challenge when teaching spelling is ensuring that pupils apply what they have learnt in spelling sessions to their own independent writing in real contexts. The 'Read–cover–write' sentences that are a feature of the pupil books are designed to help pupils make exactly that link: from practising spellings to applying their new spelling knowledge when writing.

The link can be made more explicit by having an 'Apply it in writing' session once the pupil book page has been completed. Here it is important to firmly establish the expectation that what has been taught and practised is applied when writing.

Independent writing

Where possible, the 'Apply it in writing' session should be embedded within an independent writing task planned for the week. It may feature in any area of the curriculum, not just English. Some suggestions are given in the 'Teaching notes', but ideally you should look for opportunities to embed words and apply current learning in writing you have planned for the week. For example: the rules for adding **ed** can be applied while writing a story or a recount in history; writing a list of items using plural spellings might be part of a craft session.

Embedding the spelling focus should not interrupt the focus on composition. You should use the 'Target reminder' copymasters to recap the spelling focus; explain that you will be looking to see if pupils are spelling these words correctly. It may also be helpful for pupils to have the pupil books available for reference when they are writing.

There are other opportunities for pupils to apply spelling in writing. These include:
- reviewing and proof reading their own writing
- responding to marking.

In the above activities, pupils can use their new spelling knowledge to correct errors made earlier. They can either work independently or with a partner in paired review and, again, should be encouraged to refer back to the pupil book for help.

> **Please note:** For more details about the relationship between spelling and the different stages of writing see the 'Spelling in the context of writing' section on pages 13 and 14.

Spelling sentences

There will be some occasions when writing already planned for the week will not provide a suitable opportunity to practise using a particular set of spellings. In this case, a short 'Spelling sentences' activity can be used instead. This involves giving pupils two or three target words, and possibly a theme or subject, and asking them to compose and write a sentence using those words. The activity is designed to replicate the process of drawing on spelling knowledge while composing and writing.

A 'Spelling sentences' activity could be used as a warm-up to a longer writing session, or it could be combined with work on sentence construction and punctuation. The level of challenge can be adapted for different ages and current learning. For example, you might instruct pupils to *Write a question*, or to *Write a complex sentence*.

Stage four: Assess

Assessment facilitates reflection on learning.

Regular weekly assessments are important for both teacher and pupils to reflect on learning in relation to the new focus and to check that key spellings have been learnt.

The main feature of the weekly assessment is a dictation sentence including target words from the current focus. Sometimes words introduced previously are also included to check that learning has been retained. The dictation sentence is given in the 'Teaching notes', with target words underlined. It can be shortened or lengthened if required.

A conventional spelling test may also be used, if necessary. You can simply select five to ten words from the pupil book and use these to test pupils. You may decide to include, as a challenge, one or two additional words that follow the same pattern but do not appear in the pupil book.

Using the dictation sentences

Read the dictation sentence aloud, breaking it into meaningful chunks and saying any punctuation marks. Although punctuation is not part of the assessment, pupils should be expected to include it as it helps to reinforce their understanding of punctuation and how it is used in writing. Read each chunk several times as pupils write it word for word. Encourage pupils to check what they have written.

Once the dictation is complete, write or display the sentence on the board so pupils can check their own or each other's work word by word, underlining any errors. Errors should be discussed to help pupils understand why they occurred: for example, the pupil may have forgotten a particular rule or pattern.

A 'Dictation assessment sheet' copymaster is provided in the **Teacher's Resource Book**. This has space for five dictation assessments. Completed over a number of weeks, the document becomes a useful record of performance that you and your pupils can use to discuss progress.

Reflecting on learning

Pupils should be encouraged to reflect on their learning by, for example, saying what they have learnt and how they used the new guideline or rule to spell words. The box or boxes at the bottom of the pupil book page are to be ticked when the pupil can confidently agree with the 'I can' statement. Pupils should decide when they are ready to tick each box. You might like to suggest that they use a single line only to show that a target has been partly achieved but still needs more practice (for example, in applying the rule to their own writing). The full tick can be inserted later when the learning is secure.

It is important, at this stage, that you decide whether pupils have understood the focus and learnt spellings or whether an additional session is needed to revise and recap. Even if pupils seem to have grasped the focus at this point, it is likely to need revision in future weeks. This will ensure that their learning becomes fully embedded and is used effectively when writing.

> **Please note:** To see how weekly assessments fit into the full assessment plan, see the 'Assessment and record keeping' section on pages 18 to 20.

3 Further guidelines for use

Timetabling and organising sessions

Several short and focused spelling sessions are generally found to be more effective than an occasional longer session. Below is a suggestion for how **Schofield & Sims Spelling** could be used in short daily sessions following the teach–practise–apply–assess model. You do not necessarily need to follow this model, however. **Spelling** is flexible and the materials can be used to fit with however your school organises the teaching of spelling.

DAY 1 – STAGE ONE: TEACH Use the 'Teaching notes' in this **Teacher's Guide** to introduce, demonstrate and explain the new spelling focus. Pupils write words with you.

DAY 2 – STAGE TWO: PRACTISE Pupils work independently or in pairs to complete the relevant page in the pupil book. Alternatively, you might set one of the activities as homework. Use copymasters from the **Teacher's Resource Book** to provide extension activities, if needed.

DAY 3* OR DAY 4* – STAGE THREE: APPLY Use a 'Target reminder' (available as a copymaster in the **Teacher's Resource Book**) to recap the focus. Referring to the pupil book as necessary, pupils use what they have learnt about spelling in a writing activity.

DAY 4* OR DAY 5* – STAGE FOUR: ASSESS This session encourages both assessment and reflection. Use the dictation sentence from the 'Teaching notes', plus a selection of other words if required, to test pupils' understanding. Pupils take part in paired marking and are given the opportunity to reflect on their learning.

---

*Please note: At some point during Day 3, 4 or 5 you may need to convene a revision session that aims to revisit, recap and reinforce the learning that has occurred during Stages one and two (teach and practise) or previous learning. The purpose of this session is to ensure that the spellings learnt are fully embedded.

This session can be used flexibly at any point during the week to pick up on points that you have noted. For example, it may be that after Stages one and two, pupils have not yet grasped the new guideline. If this is the case, the session can be used to reinforce teaching and give pupils extra practice before they move on to Stages three and four (apply and assess).

Alternatively, it may be that spelling errors in pupils' independent writing at Stage three (apply) suggest that revision of a previous teaching point would be useful. Use copymasters from the **Teacher's Resource Book** to introduce the guideline in a different way or using different words.

Differentiation, grouping and partner work

Differentiation

Schofield & Sims Spelling is broadly in line with National Curriculum expectations: **Spelling 1** is aimed at pupils in Year 1, with one book provided per year up to **Spelling 6** for Year 6. There is plenty of repetition and revision to constantly reinforce earlier learning. Gradual progression in learning, with no difficult transitions between books, ensures that pupils with a few specific gaps in their knowledge are soon able to catch up and then to keep up with their peers as they work through the book designed for their year.

However, pupils should always work on the book that is most appropriate to their needs and spelling ability rather than their age or year group. It is for this reason that the pupil books are numbered rather than labelled by year group. If pupils have missed crucial areas of knowledge or have been unable to grasp key concepts they will need to work on an earlier book. For example, some pupils in Year 3 who have significant gaps in their phonic knowledge, such as poor understanding of vowel phonemes, might need to work through **Spelling 1**.

Similarly, the copymasters in the **Teacher's Resource Book** provide some extension activities that will stretch your more able pupils. However, if pupils have already grasped all the guidelines and spellings introduced in a particular pupil book they should be moved on to the next book in the series.

Grouping

Any class is likely to include pupils who are at different stages, working on different pupil books, and they will need to be grouped for teaching. The teaching sessions can be staggered, so that you work with different groups on different days or at different points within a longer session. The pupil books should be completed without your help, so while some groups are working on those you can work with another group to introduce their new focus.

Working with a partner

It can be useful for pupils to have a spelling partner. This should be a pupil of similar ability. Spelling partners could work together to complete the activities in the pupil book. The discussion between partners, particularly the discussion of spelling choices, can be helpful in developing understanding.

Paired marking, where spelling partners mark each other's work, will encourage pupils to take care when checking spellings. Pupils can use the answers at the back of their books to check their partner's work.

Once spellings have been checked and learnt, spelling partners can use the lists of words on the answer pages to test each other by taking turns to choose a word for their partner to write. For younger pupils this can be made into a game, with points being scored for each word spelt correctly. Spelling partners can also test each other on words covered in previous weeks, to ensure that they have been retained.

Spelling in the context of writing

Spelling knowledge is only useful if pupils apply it in their own writing. It is vital, therefore, that what has been taught in spelling sessions is rigorously followed up in writing across the curriculum. Only in this way will spelling knowledge be transferred to independent writing.

Once taught, strategies, patterns and guidelines should be referred to on a regular basis, whatever the writing activity. This will make the links explicit and show that what is learnt in spelling should be used when writing. This referring back can take place during any of the stages in the writing process:

- composition
- proof reading and revision
- responding to marking.

Composition

A big challenge for many pupils is trying to juggle composition skills – that is, the creative task of expressing ideas in writing – with the transcriptional skill of spelling. They must use the spelling strategies and guidelines learnt to make quick decisions about how to spell words without losing the main focus, which should be on expressing their ideas.

You can help pupils to balance and manage these two skills by:

- modelling and demonstrating the process in shared writing: for example, you might refer to a spelling pattern or explain a spelling choice
- setting targets relating to a current or recent focus and stating specifically that these will apply to all the writing pupils do; you need to make this expectation absolutely clear
- reminding pupils to apply strategies, rules and conventions they have learnt – either before they begin writing or as they write in guided sessions.

Proof reading and revision

An important part of the writing process is learning to check for misspellings and to correct errors. Pupils need to be taught the specific process of proof reading their own work. From **Spelling 2** onwards, proof reading exercises are included as part of the regular 'Revision' pages in the pupil books.

The teaching notes for the 'Revision' pages explain how to model the process of proof reading, with the focus on looking for a particular type of spelling error. This focus relates to recently taught patterns and guidelines. However, you can adapt the session to focus on any current error that is noted through ongoing assessment of pupils' spelling. As well as modelling the proof reading process, this also provides an opportunity to reinforce the guideline, rule, pattern or strategy that will help the pupil to avoid similar errors in the future.

Pupils can complete the proof reading exercise in the pupil book as preparation for proof reading their own writing. Guided proof reading sessions can be used to support pupils further. For example, you might suggest, *Let's check all the words ending with **ing**.* Younger and less confident pupils can work with proof reading partners when checking their work.

Responding to marking

A clear and consistent strategy is needed for marking spelling errors found in writing across all subjects, not just in English. This marking should be focused, reflecting pupils' growing spelling knowledge by targeting misspellings of words already taught or words that follow familiar conventions or patterns. Errors should be marked (by underlining them, for example) as an indication that you expect the pupil to correct the error and practise or learn the word so that it is not misspelt again. It is usually best to limit the number of words to be corrected in a piece of writing, particularly with younger pupils: for example, five is enough for it not to be too much of a chore.

Pupils must then be given time to respond to marking by making the corrections requested. An agreed procedure should be established for how corrections are made and how the word is to be practised. The copymaster 'Responding to marking' in the **Teacher's Resource Book** provides an example of such a procedure. Schools should adapt this to fit with their own marking policies or vary it according to the age of pupils.

As well as marking errors, you should also analyse the cause of errors. Errors resulting from lack of concentration, particularly when focusing on composition, are easily corrected. Errors showing that a particular learning point has not yet been fully embedded suggest that a quick revision session may be needed. Some other errors may reveal misunderstandings or confusions. For example, a pupil who consistently writes **stoppt** rather than **stopped** has understood the rule about doubling the last consonant but has missed the point that **ed** is always added to the end of past tense verbs, regardless of the sound it makes. Misunderstandings like this need to be clarified with the individual pupil or group.

> **Links between spelling and handwriting:** Linking the teaching of spelling with handwriting can be helpful, particularly when pupils are learning a joined-up style. Practising writing digraphs, letter strings and key words can reinforce spelling patterns while also developing fluency in handwriting.

Spelling tricky words and topic words

It is in the nature of English spelling that many words do not follow expected spelling patterns or general guidelines – and this is true of many high-frequency words that we use constantly. These words are often described as 'tricky words', and they need to be learnt. Similarly, many specialist 'topic words' that pupils encounter in subjects such as maths and science have unusual spellings – often as a result of their derivation. Again, a special effort needs to be made in learning to spell them.

Schofield & Sims Spelling introduces tricky high-frequency words and subject-specific topic words alongside the main spelling focus. Each section of a pupil book ends with either a 'Tricky words' page or a 'Topic words' page. These pages do not necessarily need to be left to the end of the section. They could be introduced earlier and then worked on over a period of weeks. With younger pupils, you might consider introducing just two words at a time.

The words featured on the 'Tricky words' or 'Topic words' pages are a selection of typical words suitable for that stage. There is also space for pupils to add a few words of their own on some pages. However, you will find blank copymaster versions of the 'Tricky words' and 'Topic words' pages in the **Teacher's Resource Book**. Either you or your pupils can use these to create customised lists of words – whether they relate to specific topics or to words that currently seem troublesome.

The 'Tricky words' and 'Topic words' pages have been designed to help pupils become familiar with a routine for learning such spellings. This routine, as outlined below, should be taught, demonstrated and discussed regularly, as described in the 'Teaching notes', so that pupils become familiar with it. A copymaster version of this routine appears in the **Teacher's Resource Book**; you can use this as a focus for discussion, then leave it on display in the classroom or give it to pupils to keep in their spelling journals.

Once tricky and topic words have been taught, it is important to establish a clear expectation that they should be spelt correctly in independent writing and to follow this up in marking. 'Mini-targets' should be set using the 'Target reminder 3' in the **Teacher's Resource Book** and pupils encouraged to monitor their own progress towards the target. For example, they might add a tick each time the word is spelt correctly. A word could be considered learnt once it has been spelt correctly five times in independent writing.

Alternatively, current tricky words or topic words could be displayed on word lists for pupils to refer to as they write. As pupils begin to spell the words correctly in independent writing, these prompts can be taken down to see if pupils retain and continue to use the correct spelling.

Teaching strategies

Always establish that not the entire word is tricky. Show that, once broken down, most parts of a word are spelt as they sound or follow known spelling patterns. There are usually just one or two tricky bits that need special attention.

1. TAKE THE WORD APART With shorter words, say the sounds as you write the corresponding letters. With longer words, first say the syllables and then say the sounds for each syllable in turn. Alternatively, longer words can be separated into root words and affixes and recorded as a 'word sum'.

2. IDENTIFY THE TRICKY PART Compare the sounds with the letters. Find the part of the word with the unexpected spelling. Circle it, or write it in a different colour to show that this is the part that needs to be learnt.

3. CHOOSE A MEMORY STRATEGY The memory strategy will help pupils to remember the correct spelling of the word and its tricky bit. Over time, introduce pupils to a range of memory strategies, for example:

- *Say it as it's spelt* – rather than saying the word as it is normally pronounced: for example, say *w-a-s* (not *w-o-s*) or *k-nock* (pronouncing the silent **k**) rather than nock.

- *Say the syllables* – say all the syllables clearly and distinctly, rather than as pronounced normally, to help pupils to write the unstressed parts of words: for example, *Wed/nes/day*.

- *Chant the letter names* – say the letter names as you write the word or the tricky part of a longer word: for example, *o-u-t spells out*.

- *Spell it like . . .* – make a link to another word with the same spelling pattern and write the words together: for example, **could**, **would**.

- *Use a memory trick*: for example, find a word within a word to fix the spelling in your head (for example, *piece of pie*) or make up a mnemonic (for example: **could**, **should**, **would** – <u>O</u> <u>U</u> Look <u>Divine</u>; or **rhyme** – <u>R</u>hyme <u>H</u>elps <u>Y</u>ou and <u>ME</u>).

4. TRY IT Follow this simple routine:

- *cover* the word

- *write* it (using a memory strategy)

- *check* it

and repeat as necessary.

5. KEEP PRACTISING . . . to make sure it sticks.

Different practice strategies for different learning styles

Not everyone learns in the same way, so, as well as using the different teaching strategies described above, it is a good idea to introduce a varied range of practice strategies over time. Encourage pupils to try out different strategies in order to discover which work best for them. Examples of two possible strategies are given below.

VISUAL STRATEGIES These involve picturing the word, becoming accustomed to its shape and the patterns made by the letters. Ask pupils to look at the word repeatedly. Then cover it while pupils still visualise it. After a short time, ask pupils to write the word and check whether they think it looks right. Finally, reveal the word and ask pupils to check theirs against the correct spelling.

KINAESTHETIC STRATEGIES These involve pupils getting a 'feel' for writing the word and learning the hand movements needed to write it until writing it correctly becomes automatic. Encourage pupils to trace words in the air or on paper, or ask them to write them repeatedly, using joined-up handwriting.

Supporting teaching and learning

The **Teacher's Resource Book** includes a range of general copymasters that support teaching and learning by providing templates for the following, with full instructions for use:

- extension and revision activities

- prompts and reminders.

Copymasters for extension and revision activities

The purpose of these activities is to reinforce or extend learning points that are first introduced in the pupil books.

During the week in which a particular focus is introduced, the copymasters can be used to create extension or challenge activities for more able pupils. For example, these might require pupils to carry out investigations or apply guidelines to other words. In subsequent weeks, the activities can be used to revise or reinforce a focus. For example, you might revise a guideline or rule, introducing it in a different way or with different words.

The extension and revision copymasters include the following items.

ADDITIONAL WORD LISTS These feature more words that follow the same rule, guideline or spelling pattern, extending the range that is provided in the pupil book. Use them to give pupils the opportunity to explore or investigate patterns further or to provide them with more practice in applying rules and guidelines. The lists can be used in conjunction with the 'Word sort' copymasters described below or in partner games such as 'Partner challenge', 'Find a friend' or 'Describe the word' (see below).

SPELLING LOGS 'Spelling log 1' folds up to make a small booklet that pupils can keep with them when writing. Pupils select a small number of words they think will be useful in their writing, and then make an effort to learn them. The words might relate to a particular spelling pattern or formation: for example, words with suffixes. Pupils tick the word each time it is used successfully in their writing. This activity can also encourage pupils to use more adventurous words in their own compositions.

WORD SORT COPYMASTERS These can be used to investigate or reinforce rules and spelling patterns: for example, investigating different spellings of a vowel phoneme or rules for adding suffixes. Pupils sort words from a given word list, or words they find in a book, according to spelling patterns; they then record the words in the correct box.

WORD COLLECTOR COPYMASTERS These are used to explore words with particular spelling patterns. Pupils search books or a dictionary for words with a given spelling pattern and record them on the sheets.

WORDS TO PRACTISE: SPELLING PRACTICE LADDERS This copymaster provides a reinforcement activity to practise spelling words that need special attention. These might include, for example, words that are spelt wrongly in the weekly dictation or words that are marked as incorrect in independent writing. Pupils write the word correctly and then practise it by saying and writing it a number of times.

Some of the copymasters are particularly well suited to partner games, as follows.

PARTNER CHALLENGE Both partners are given time to study a list of words with a particular spelling pattern. They then take it in turns to be the challenger who chooses one of the words from the list and says it in a sentence. The challenged partner writes it down without looking at the list. Both partners check the spelling together and agree the points scored: for example, one point for the correct spelling of a short word and one point for each syllable spelt correctly in a longer word.

FIND A FRIEND A set of words is cut up to make individual word cards. Partners take it in turns to pick a word and then 'Find a friend' from the remaining words that shares the same spelling pattern. To score a point, the picker must point out to their partner the shared pattern or feature that links the words.

DESCRIBE THE WORD Both partners have the same list of words. They take it in turns to describe the features of a word without actually saying it. The partner has to work out which word is being described.

Copymasters that provide prompts and reminders

The purpose of these sheets is to help pupils remember spelling strategies, key learning points and routines. All of these should first be discussed with the class, and the routines and strategies modelled so they become established as basic classroom practice.

Copies of the prompts and reminders can then be displayed in the classroom, given to pupils or stuck in spelling journals and exercise books for pupils to use at appropriate times.

The prompts and reminders include the following items.

TARGET REMINDERS These can be used to set expectations that apply to all pupils' writing, in any part of the school curriculum or when they write at home.

LEARNING AND PRACTISING TRICKY WORDS These provide strategies for learning tricky high-frequency words.

SPELLING STRATEGIES TO USE WHEN WRITING These provide strategies that will help pupils to attempt words that they are not sure of as they are writing.

RESPONDING TO MARKING PROMPTS These help pupils to establish a routine for correcting spelling errors.

Assessment and record keeping

The purpose of spelling assessment is to find out what pupils know and what they need to know, so as to inform planning and teaching. **Schofield & Sims Spelling** incorporates a layered assessment plan of ongoing and periodic assessment, as summarised below.

Ongoing assessment   → pupil book, all independent writing

Ongoing self-assessment   → pupil book, target reminder sheets

Weekly assessment task   → dictation and spelling test

Periodic assessment   → printed cloze-style spelling tests

                            → error analysis sheet.

Ongoing assessment

The pupil book and independent writing across the curriculum provide plenty of opportunities to assess how well pupils have grasped the rules, guidelines, patterns and strategies being taught. When marking independent writing, you need to be aware of both the current focus and earlier spellings to check that they have been retained and are being used effectively.

> **Please note:** Problems noted during your marking of the pupil books and pupils' independent writing should be followed up in the weekly revision session. They must not be left unaddressed.

Ongoing self-assessment

The 'I can' statements at the bottom of each page of the pupil book encourage pupils to continually monitor their learning. From **Spelling 3** onwards, two statements are given: pupils need first to decide if they can spell the words in the pupil book and, second, to decide whether they are confident about applying the basic rule or guideline in their own writing. Pupils do not have to tick the statements immediately: they may be ticked at a later date.

Self-assessment is also encouraged through targets set on the 'Target reminder' copymasters. These are wider targets to be worked on over a half term and should apply to all the writing that pupils do, across the curriculum. They are most likely to be group or class targets. The target is recorded and pupils note down evidence of achieving the target over time. There is also space for you to write a comment: for example, at the end of the half term.

In addition to the main target, individual pupils may be set a mini-target, which relates to specific words that they find difficult. 'Target reminder 3' has space for words to be listed and for the pupil to tick them each time they are spelt correctly in his or her writing.

Weekly assessment task

This is a focused assessment provided in the assessment section of the 'Teaching notes'. It is usually in the form of a dictation sentence designed to check that pupils have grasped the current learning point and learnt to spell words from the pupil book. Please note that dictation sentences sometimes include previously taught words to check that they have been retained. If appropriate, you can also select five to 10 words from the relevant page in the pupil book and give a short additional spelling test.

However, you should not rely purely on the weekly spelling test to assess whether pupils have learnt spellings and understood guidelines. Pupils often learn a correct spelling in the short term but, without regular practice, they may not retain it. Ongoing assessment of independent writing will show whether learning has been embedded and is being applied or if further reinforcement is needed in a revision session.

Periodic assessment

Three longer cloze-style spelling tests are provided for each pupil book in the form of a 'Dictation test', one for each term. Use the appropriate test for the term; you do not need to use all three. The tests cover a range of words representing cumulative learning to that point and provide a more objective view of what each pupil knows in relation to expected progress. Each test assesses between 10 and 20 words and consists of a cloze-style passage with target words to be written in as they are read aloud. Full instructions and all the resources for these assessments can be found in the **Teacher's Resource Book**.

'Error analysis sheets' are provided for the periodic dictation tests. Marking words or parts of words that have been spelt incorrectly will help you to identify individual or group weaknesses and find areas that need to be revisited. You can use this information to adjust future planning and teaching: for example, deciding on a focus for a revision week.

An 'Error analysis sheet' is also provided to help you assess spelling within samples of independent writing. This formal analysis of independent writing only needs to be done occasionally and is not usually necessary for all pupils. It can be helpful, however, in identifying areas that are particularly problematic for pupils who are struggling. Discussion with the pupil about why he or she made a particular spelling choice can help explain the cause of problems and will enable you to set individual targets.

Record keeping

A 'Target and progress tracking sheet' is provided in the **Teacher's Resource Book** for recording progress in relation to key objectives. There is space for you to record evidence from the weekly assessment task and from the ongoing assessment of writing.

The 'Target and progress tracking sheet', together with the following materials, will build up a spelling portfolio:

● weekly 'Dictation assessment sheets', completed by the pupil

● completed 'Target reminder' sheets (dated, with comments from you and the pupil)

● annotated samples of writing (for example, showing use of a particular rule)

● cloze-style tests, marked and analysed.

4 Scope and sequence

Book 1 scope and sequence

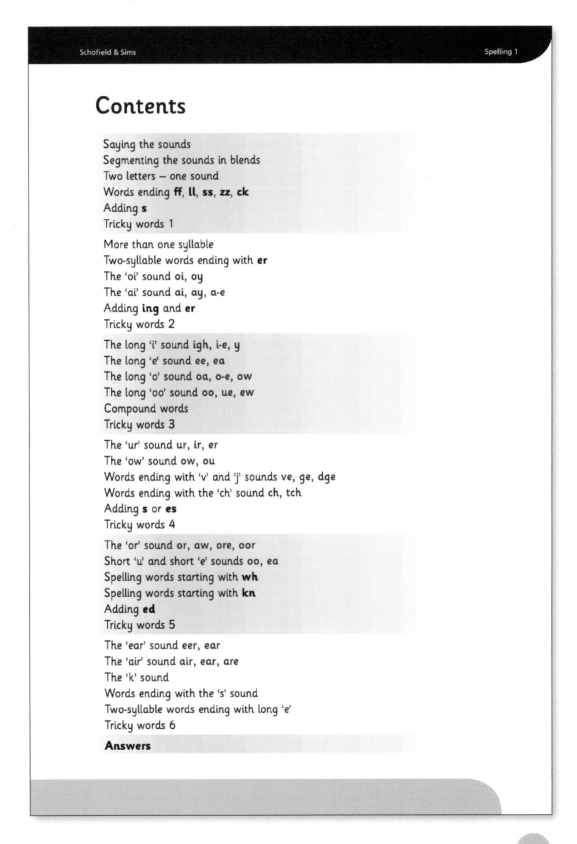

Schofield & Sims   Spelling 1

Contents

Saying the sounds
Segmenting the sounds in blends
Two letters — one sound
Words ending **ff**, **ll**, **ss**, **zz**, **ck**
Adding **s**
Tricky words 1

More than one syllable
Two-syllable words ending with **er**
The 'oi' sound oi, oy
The 'ai' sound ai, ay, a-e
Adding **ing** and **er**
Tricky words 2

The long 'i' sound igh, i-e, y
The long 'e' sound ee, ea
The long 'o' sound oa, o-e, ow
The long 'oo' sound oo, ue, ew
Compound words
Tricky words 3

The 'ur' sound ur, ir, er
The 'ow' sound ow, ou
Words ending with 'v' and 'j' sounds ve, ge, dge
Words ending with the 'ch' sound ch, tch
Adding **s** or **es**
Tricky words 4

The 'or' sound or, aw, ore, oor
Short 'u' and short 'e' sounds oo, ea
Spelling words starting with **wh**
Spelling words starting with **kn**
Adding **ed**
Tricky words 5

The 'ear' sound eer, ear
The 'air' sound air, ear, are
The 'k' sound
Words ending with the 's' sound
Two-syllable words ending with long 'e'
Tricky words 6

Answers

Book 2 scope and sequence

Contents

The long 'a' sound
The long 'i' sound
The long 'o' sound
The long 'e' sound
The long 'oo' sound
Tricky words 1 **exceptions to long vowel spellings**

Adding **ing**
Adding **ed**
Doubling letters before **ing** and **ed**
Adding **ing** and **ed** to words ending **y**
Revision 1 **long vowels, compound words and verb endings**
Tricky words 2 **different spellings of the 'u' sound**

Adding **s** and **es**
Adding **s** to words ending **y**
The **w** special
The **q** special
Soft **g** where **g** makes a 'j' sound
Tricky words 3

Adding the suffix **y**
Adding **er** and **est**
Adding **ful** and **less**
Words that sound the same
Revision 2 **compound words and adding suffixes**
Topic words 1 **story writing**

Adding the prefix **un**
Adding the prefixes **un** and **dis**
Tricky consonants 1 **ph** and **ch**
Tricky consonants 2 **kn, wr, mb**
Soft **c** where **c** makes a 's' sound
Topic words 2 **days of the week**

Two-syllable words
Words ending 'shun' and 'ul'
Taking words apart
Shortened forms
Revision 3 **new graphemes and endings**
Tricky words 4

Answers

Book 3 scope and sequence

Contents

Words ending **le**
Double letters before **le**
Double letters before other endings
Words ending **el**, **al** and **il**
More word endings
Topic words 1 months of the year

Adding **ed**
Adding **ed** and **ing** to words ending **y**
Irregular past tense
Adding **s** and **es**
Revision 1 rules for adding **ed** and **le** endings
Topic words 2 maths

Spelling patterns: **c** and **k**
Spelling patterns: **x** and **ex**
More 'or' spellings
More 'ur' spellings
More 'oo' and 'yoo' spellings
Topic words 3 describing words

Adding **y**
Adding **er** and **est**
Adding **ly**
Spelling words with suffixes **ful**, **less**, **able**, **ness**, **ment**, **er**
Revision 2 rules for adding suffixes
Topic words 4 science

Shortened forms 1 contractions with pronouns
Shortened forms 2 other contractions
Silent letters
Soft **g** and soft **c**
Homophones
Topic words 5 English

Prefixes: **re**, **de**, **pre** and **mis**
More prefixes
Words ending **ture** and **sure**
Possessive apostrophes
Revision 3 **ture** and **sure**, prefixes, silent letters
Tricky words

Answers

Book 4 scope and sequence

Contents

Homophones 1
Homophones 2
The **ch** grapheme 'k' and 'sh' sounds
Y as a vowel
The apostrophe test
Tricky words

Tricky plurals 1
Tricky plurals 2
Spelling patterns **gu** and **gue**
Spelling patterns **qu** and **que**
Revision 1 new spelling patterns, homophones
Topic words 1 maths

Letter strings: **ear**
Letter strings: **gh**
Prefixes **al**, **a**, **ad** and **be**
Detecting prefixes
Adding **ly**
Topic words 2 science

Adding **ed** and **ing**
Adjective suffixes **al**, **ic**, **able** and **ive**
Verb suffixes **ise**, **ify**, **ate** and **en**
Forming nouns vowel and consonant suffixes
Revision 2 rules for adding suffixes and prefixes
Topic words 3 geography

Adding **ation**
Words ending 'shun' **tion**, **sion** and **ssion**
Words ending **ous** and **ious**
Words ending **able** and **ible**
The possessive apostrophe: plurals
Topic words 4 English

Say the syllables
Detecting roots and affixes
Word families
Greek and Latin prefixes
Revision 3 word endings and linked words
Topic words 5 school subjects

Answers

Book 5 scope and sequence

Schofield & Sims

Spelling 5

Contents

Unstressed vowels 1 say the syllables
Unstressed vowels 2 word structure
Words ending 'er' **er**, **ar**, **or** and **re**
Words ending **ary**, **ory** and **ery**
Words ending 'shun' **tion**, **cian**, **sion** and **ssion**
Tricky words

Letter string **au**
Letter string **our**
Letter string **ough**
Words with **ie** and **ei**
Revision 1
Topic words 1 geography

Words with soft **c**
Spelling patterns **ci**, **cu** and **cc**
Words with soft **g**
Silent letters
Words ending **ti** and **tu**
Topic words 2 science

Prefixes **in**, **im**, **ir** and **il**
More **ad** prefixes
Detecting prefixes and roots
Homophones
Revision 2
Topic words 3 maths

Adding suffixes: words ending **e**
Adding suffixes: words ending **y**
Adding suffixes: double the last letter
Words ending **ous**
Words ending **able** and **ible**
Topic words 4 English

Word structure
Word families
Word histories
Common confusions
Revision 3
Personal spelling list

Answers

Book 6 scope and sequence

Contents

Representing sounds
Building words with affixes
Rules and exceptions adding **ly**
Word relationships
Visual strategies
Tricky words 1 connectives and adverbs

Unstressed vowels
Unstressed consonants
Unstressed endings: **ant**, **ance**, **ent**, **ence**
Double or single consonants
Revision 1 word endings
Tricky words 2 foreign imports

Prefixes to support spelling
Choosing the correct prefix
Hyphens
Common confusions 1 **Noun or verb**?
Homophones and near homophones
Topic words 1 history

Adding suffixes to words ending **l**
Adding suffixes to words ending **fer**
Adding **ate**, **ify**, **ise** and **en**
Changes to root words
Revision 2 affixes
Topic words 2 English

Word families
Latin and Greek roots
Formation of words
Greek spelling patterns **ph**, **hy**, **rh**, **ps** and **pn**
Word endings
Topic words 3 maths

Common confusions 2 Which is it?
Common confusions 3 One word or two?
People and places
Using a dictionary
Revision 3
Personal spelling list

Answers

5 Teaching notes

Spelling 1

Spelling 1   page 4

FOCUS Saying the sounds

TEACH ▶ Recap segmenting sounds in words. Say a three-letter word (for example, **bag**). Say the three sounds, counting them on your fingers. Let pupils say the sounds as you write the letters. ▶ Say another word (for example, **run**). Ask pupils to say the sounds and then, with a partner, write and show the letters. ▶ Repeat with other words covering a variety of letters (for example, **tin**, **hop**, **yes**, **fix**). ▶ Look for sounds and letters that are being confused. Revise the letter that represents the sound and give another word with the same letter/sound.

PRACTISE Spelling 1, page 4; 'Additional word list'

APPLY Set target; independent writing

ASSESS Dictation: <u>Red</u> <u>fox</u> has a <u>bad</u> <u>leg</u>.

Spelling 1   page 5

FOCUS Segmenting the sounds in blends

TEACH ▶ Say a CCVC word (for example, **stop**). Say and count the phonemes (**s-t-o-p**). ▶ Explain that **s** and **t** blend together when said normally, but must be separated out to spell the word. Demonstrate saying the word with the sounds clearly distinguished. Ask pupils to do this as you write the letters. ▶ Say other CCVC words so pupils, in pairs, can say and count the sounds. ▶ Repeat with a CVCC word (for example, **went**). This time demonstrate saying the individual consonant sounds at the end (**n-t**). ▶ Ask pupils to do the same with **jump**.

PRACTISE Spelling 1, page 5; 'Additional word list'

APPLY Set target; independent writing; respond to marking

ASSESS Dictation: A big dog <u>went</u> to <u>jump</u> in the <u>sand</u>.

Spelling 1   page 6

FOCUS Two letters – one sound

TEACH ▶ Say the word **fish**. Ask pupils to say and count the sounds (**f-i-sh**). ▶ Draw three dots to represent the three sounds. Write the corresponding letters above the dots as pupils say the sound. ▶ Explain that the sound 'sh' needs two letters (**sh**). ▶ Ask pupils to say the sounds and write and show another **sh** word (for example, **shop**). ▶ Recap other sounds that need two letters: **ch**, **th**, **ar**, **or**. Say the sound and ask pupils to write it. ▶ Support pupils to say the sounds and write words such as **chop**, **thin**, **hard**, **sort**.

PRACTISE Spelling 1, page 6; 'Additional word list'

APPLY Independent writing; paired review

ASSESS Dictation: **I must <u>rush</u> to the <u>shop</u> in the <u>car</u>.**

Spelling 1   page 7

FOCUS Words ending **ff**, **ll**, **ss**, **zz**, **ck**

TEACH ▶ Revise segmenting sounds to spell words. Ask pupils to write and show: **wet**, **frog**, **thin**. ▶ Check that each sound is represented by the right letter or letters. ▶ Say **bell**. Together, say and count the sounds (**b-e-ll**). ▶ Draw three dots to represent the three sounds. Write the letters above the dots as pupils say the sound. ▶ Explain that at the end of a short word after **a**, **e**, **i**, **o** and **u** a 'l' sound is spelt **ll**. ▶ Ask pupils to write **sell**. ▶ Repeat with the words **hiss**, **off**, **buzz**, **neck**. ▶ Establish that the same thing happens with **s**, **f** and **z** and that in the case of a 'k' sound the spelling is **ck**.

PRACTISE Spelling 1, page 7; 'Additional word list'

APPLY Independent writing; paired review

ASSESS Dictation: **The <u>duck</u> <u>fell</u> <u>off</u> the <u>back</u>.**

Spelling 1 page 8

FOCUS Adding s

TEACH ▶ Say nouns for pupils to write and show (for example, **ship**, **step**, **car**). ▶ Write a list of the words on the board so pupils can check their spellings. ▶ Recap previous teaching points (for example: segmenting sounds; writing appropriate letter or letters). ▶ Add the number two in front of each word on the board. ▶ Read the new list together, orally adding the s to make the words into plurals. ▶ Demonstrate adding s to change the spellings. ▶ Establish that if there is more than one of something you add s to the end of the word. ▶ Ask pupils to write **frogs**.

PRACTISE Spelling 1, page 8; 'Additional word list'

APPLY Spelling sentences; independent writing (for example, list of items)

ASSESS Dictation: **He <u>claps</u> his <u>hands</u> and <u>swings</u> his <u>arms</u>.**

Spelling 1 page 9

FOCUS Tricky words 1

TEACH ▶ Select two words from the list that pupils find difficult. Write one on the board (for example, **was**) and say it in a sentence. ▶ Say the sounds as you point to the letters in the word. ▶ Identify the tricky letter. ▶ Ask why errors are made (for example, in **was**, **a** is not the usual spelling for the 'o' sound). ▶ Discuss ways to remember the correct spelling, for example, say it as it's spelt (w-a-s). ▶ Ask pupils to say this a few times and to trace the word with their finger. ▶ Cover the word. ▶ Ask pupils to write and show: **I was** lost. ▶ Check spellings. ▶ Repeat the procedure with another word.

PRACTISE Spelling 1, page 9; 'Words to practise: My tricky words'

APPLY Set mini-targets; independent writing; paired review or respond to marking

ASSESS Dictation: **<u>She</u> will <u>be</u> so glad <u>that</u> <u>he</u> can <u>go</u>.**

Spelling 1 page 10

FOCUS More than one syllable

TEACH ▶ Say two-syllable words and clap the syllables or beats (for example, **fin/ish**, **chil/dren**). ▶ Draw a line for each syllable as pupils say the syllables (for example, **chil/dren**). ▶ Demonstrate saying the sounds and writing the first syllable (**ch-i-l**) and then the second (**d-r-e-n**). ▶ Establish the importance of saying the second syllable clearly to get the right sounds and spell it correctly (<u>chil-dren</u>). ▶ Let pupils use the same routine to say and write the word. ▶ Repeat the routine with a word ending **ing**, (for example, **telling**, **buzzing**). Demonstrate saying the **ing** ending clearly so it is easier to spell.

PRACTISE Spelling 1, page 10; 'Additional word list'

APPLY Guided and independent writing

ASSESS Dictation: **The <u>children</u> will <u>visit</u> in the <u>morning</u>.**

Spelling 1 page 11

FOCUS Two-syllable words ending with er

TEACH ▶ Recap the routine for spelling two-syllable words. Say **thun/der** and clap the beats or syllables. ▶ Together, say the sounds in the first syllable as you write **th-u-n** and then in the second as you write **d-er**. ▶ Write over **er** in colour. Explain that **er** is the spelling for this sound at the end of words. ▶ Use the same routine to write other examples (for example, **corner**, **better**). ▶ Show how to stress the second syllable and say the 'er' sound clearly (for example, **cor/<u>ner</u>**) to get the correct spelling and avoid errors such as **corna** and **betta**.

PRACTISE Spelling 1, page 11; 'Additional word list'

APPLY Independent writing or spelling sentences

ASSESS Dictation: **I <u>never</u> <u>ever</u> get a <u>number</u> <u>under</u> seven.**

Spelling 1   page 12

FOCUS The 'oi' sound

TEACH ▶ Show flashcards of **oy** and **oi** to establish that both represent the same sound. ▶ Explain that good spellers know how to choose the right spelling for a word. ▶ Say **boy**. Say the sounds and write **b-oy** on the board. Write over **oy** in colour. ▶ Repeat with the word **boil** (b-oi-l), writing over **oi**. ▶ Use rhyme to generate more words with the 'oi' sound at the end and then in the middle (for example, **toy**, **Roy**; **soil**, **foil**). ▶ Say the sounds and write the new words under **oy** or **oi**. ▶ Discuss the pattern. Establish that the **oy** spelling is used at the end of words (or syllables) and **oi** in the middle. ▶ Ask pupils to write **coin**. Discuss how they knew which **oi** spelling to use.

PRACTISE Spelling 1, page 12; 'Word sort 1'

APPLY Spelling sentences

ASSESS Dictation: **The <u>boy</u> dug up a silver <u>coin</u> from the <u>soil</u>.**

Spelling 1   page 13

FOCUS The 'ai' sound

TEACH ▶ Say the sounds and write **day** (d-ay), **pain** (p-ai-n) and **make** (m-a-k-e). Underline the three long 'a' spellings (**ay**, **ai**, **a-e**). ▶ Discuss other words with a long 'a' sound. Say the sounds and write them on the board, grouping them according to the spelling. (If suggested, group words with alternative spellings as tricky words, for example, **they**.) ▶ Discuss patterns that will help to make good spelling choices, for example: **ay** at the end of words (or syllables); **a-e** more common than **ai**; groups of words with spelling patterns such as **ake**, **ave**, **ame**, **ape**, **ain**. Establish that pupils can use these patterns to help them choose the right 'ai' spelling in words.

PRACTISE Spelling 1, page 13; 'Additional word list'

APPLY Set target; independent writing

ASSESS Dictation: **We <u>came</u> to <u>play</u> a <u>game</u> but <u>may</u> not <u>stay</u> if it <u>rains</u>.**

Spelling 1   page 14

FOCUS Adding **ing** and **er**

TEACH ▶ Say a list of verbs for pupils to write (for example, **help**, **paint**, **play**). Write the list on the board so pupils can check their spellings. ▶ Go down the list orally adding **ing**. For example, say: *I am painting.* ▶ Explain that **ing** adds an extra syllable and add **ing** to the words on the board. Let pupils do the same on their list. ▶ Rub off the **ing** endings and go down the list orally adding **er**. For example, say: *I am a painter.* ▶ Explain that **er** adds an extra syllable and add **er** to the words on the board. ▶ Ask pupils to write the word **player**.

PRACTISE Spelling 1, page 14; 'Additional word list'

APPLY Paired review; respond to marking

ASSESS Dictation: **The <u>player</u> is <u>hanging</u> his <u>jumper</u> on the peg.**

Spelling 1   page 15

FOCUS Tricky words 2

TEACH ▶ Select two words pupils find difficult. Write one on the board (for example, **they**) and say it in a sentence. ▶ Say the sounds as you point to the appropriate letters in the word. Identify the tricky bit and discuss why errors are made (for example, **thay** – **ey** is not the usual spelling for that sound). ▶ Discuss a way to remember the correct spelling (for example, *Looks like the*). ▶ Ask pupils to practise saying and writing **the** and then adding **y**. ▶ Cover the word and ask pupils to write: **They** can help. ▶ Check spellings and repeat with another word.

PRACTISE Spelling 1, page 15; 'Words to practise: My tricky words'

APPLY Set mini-targets; independent writing; respond to marking

ASSESS Dictation: **<u>They</u> <u>said</u> <u>they</u> <u>like</u> to <u>have</u> cake.**

Spelling 1   page 16

FOCUS The long 'i' sound

TEACH ▶ Say the sounds and write the words **my**, **like**, **light**. ▶ Underline the long 'i' spellings (**y**, **i-e**, **igh**). ▶ Say more words (for example, **fly**, **bike**, **might**). Ask pupils to say the sounds and help you choose the right spelling for the long 'i' sound. Use this to encourage reasoned choices rather than guessing randomly. ▶ Group the words according to the spelling and discuss patterns that help to make good spelling choices, for example: **y** at the end of a word; **igh** if followed by **t**; **i-e** is the most common spelling when the 'i' sound is followed by other letters (for example, **ine**, **ike**, **ide** and **ile**).

PRACTISE Spelling 1, page 16; 'Additional word list'

APPLY Set target; independent writing

ASSESS Dictation: **I will <u>try</u> painting a <u>bright</u> <u>line</u> on the <u>side</u> of my <u>bike</u>.**

Spelling 1   page 17

FOCUS The long 'e' sound

TEACH ▶ Write **ee** and **ea** on the board. Establish that both make the long 'ee' sound. ▶ Say the word **eat**. Write __**t**. Demonstrate writing **eat** and **eet**. Ask which looks right. ▶ Establish the correct spelling (**eat**) and quickly rub off the incorrect one. ▶ Say a series of linked words and ask pupils to write them (for example, **eat**, **seat**, **heat**) to help fix a group of words that share the same spelling pattern. ▶ Repeat the process, starting with the word **keep** and then writing a series of linked words (for example, **deep**, **weep**, **sleep**).

PRACTISE Spelling 1, page 17; 'Additional word list'; 'Word sort 1'

APPLY Set target; independent writing

ASSESS Dictation: <u>Each</u> <u>sheep</u> <u>eats</u> <u>green</u> grass <u>three</u> times a <u>week</u>.

Spelling 1   page 18

FOCUS The long 'o' sound

TEACH ▶ Sound spell and write on the board: **snow**, **woke** and **boat**. ▶ Underline the long 'o' spelling in each word (**ow**, **o-e**, **oa**). ▶ Ask pupils to suggest other words with this sound. ▶ Say the sounds and write these on the board, grouping them according to the spelling. Have a separate group for any words with alternative spellings (for example, **go**). ▶ Discuss patterns that will help pupils make spelling choices, for example: **ow** at the end of words; **o-e** or **oa** in the middle; more **o-e** words than **oa**; useful groups of words to learn (for example, **oke**, **ose**, **ope**; **oat**, **oad**, **oaf**).

PRACTISE Spelling 1, page 18; 'Additional word list'

APPLY Set target; independent writing

ASSESS Dictation: **I <u>hope</u> the <u>yellow</u> <u>boat</u> is not <u>slow</u> to <u>go</u> <u>home</u>.**

Spelling 1   page 19

FOCUS The long 'oo' sound

TEACH ▶ Ask pupils to write and show: **food**, **room**, **zoo**. ▶ Check spellings. Recap **oo** spelling for the 'oo' sound. ▶ Say a familiar word with an alternative 'oo' spelling (for example, **June**). Say the sounds and write **J-u-n-e**. ▶ Use colour to write over **u-e**. Explain that this is another spelling for the 'oo' sound. ▶ Discuss words that rhyme with **zoo**/end with the 'oo' sound (for example, **chew**, **grew**, **blue**). Write **choo**, **bloo** and **groo**. Do they look right? ▶ Quickly rub off **oo**. Explain that if a word ends with an 'oo' sound the most likely spelling is **ue** or **ew**. ▶ Discuss the correct spelling for the words on the board and write them in.

PRACTISE Spelling 1, page 19; 'Word sort 3'

APPLY Set target; independent writing

ASSESS Dictation: <u>Zoom</u>. Up <u>flew</u> the plane into the <u>blue</u> sky.

Spelling 1   page 20

FOCUS Compound words

TEACH ▶ Say some compound words and clap the two beats (for example, **pancake**, **daylight**). ▶ Explain that these are compound words and that they are made up of two simple words joined together. ▶ Demonstrate spelling a compound word by splitting it into its two parts and spelling each word in turn. ▶ Ask pupils to follow the same routine to write other examples, such as **teaspoon** and **playtime**.

PRACTISE Spelling 1, page 20; 'Additional word list'; 'Word collector'

APPLY Independent writing or spelling sentences

ASSESS Dictation: **It is <u>playtime</u> in the <u>farmyard</u> this <u>afternoon</u>.**

Spelling 1   page 21

FOCUS Tricky words 3

TEACH ▶ Select two words pupils frequently spell incorrectly. ▶ Say one of the words in a sentence (for example, *I went out.*). Ask pupils to have a go at writing the word. ▶ Discuss the tricky part and why errors were or might be made (for example, **owt**). ▶ Write the correct spelling on the board and discuss a memory strategy (for example, say: *o-u-t spells out*). ▶ Ask pupils to practise saying this as they trace the word with their finger. ▶ Cover the word and ask pupils to write: I went **out**. Check it. ▶ Repeat with another word.

PRACTISE Spelling 1, page 21; 'Words to practise: My tricky words'

APPLY Set mini-targets; independent writing; respond to marking

ASSESS Dictation: **She can <u>do</u> <u>most</u> things <u>here</u>.**

Spelling 1   page 22

FOCUS The 'ur' sound

TEACH ▶ Say the words **fur**, **girl** and **her**. ▶ Say the sounds and write the words (**f-ur**, **g-ir-l**, **h-er**). ▶ Establish the three different spellings of the 'ur' sound. Write over them in colour. ▶ Explain that this is a tricky spelling with several patterns. It is important to learn which spelling is used in each word and then check that it looks right. ▶ Give pupils time to look at the words on the board, saying the sounds and tracing the letters with their finger. ▶ Cover the words and say each one so pupils can write it. ▶ Remind them to look at their spellings to check if they look right. ▶ Reveal the words so they can be checked.

PRACTISE Spelling 1, page 22; 'Word sort 2'

APPLY Spelling sentences

ASSESS Dictation: **The <u>girl</u> with <u>curls</u> has on a red <u>skirt</u> and a blue <u>shirt</u>.**

Spelling 1   page 23

FOCUS The 'ow' sound

TEACH ▶ Sound spell and write on the board: **down**, **out**, **how**. Underline the two spellings of the 'ow' sound (**ow** and **ou**). ▶ Say other words with this sound (for example, **shout**, **frown**, **cow**). ▶ Ask pupils to say the sounds and help you choose the right spelling for the 'ow' sound. ▶ Encourage them to make reasoned choices rather than guessing (for example, *Shout is like out*). ▶ Group the words according to the spelling and discuss patterns that help to make good spelling choices, for example: **ow** not **ou** at the end of words; groups of words that follow a pattern (**out**, **oud**, **own**).

PRACTISE Spelling 1, page 23; 'Additional word list'

APPLY Spelling sentences or independent writing

ASSESS Dictation: **The <u>clown</u> fell <u>down</u> on the <u>ground</u> with a <u>loud</u> <u>shout</u>.**

Spelling 1   page 24

FOCUS Words ending with 'v' and 'j' sounds

TEACH ▶ Say the sounds and write the word **have** on the board (**h-a-ve**). ▶ Explain that a 'v' sound at the end of a word is spelt **ve**, not **v**. ▶ Ask pupils to write and show **give**. ▶ Say the sounds and write the word **large** (**l-ar-ge**). ▶ Explain that a 'j' sound at the end of a word is not spelt **j**. It is spelt **ge** after a long vowel sound (like **ar**). ▶ Move your hands apart to illustrate the long vowel sound in **l-ar-ge**. ▶ Ask pupils to write and show **charge**. ▶ Say the sounds and write the word **nudge**. ▶ Explain that if the 'j' sound comes straight after a short vowel (a, e, i, o, u) sound it is spelt **dge**. ▶ Ask pupils to write and show **badge**.

PRACTISE **Spelling 1**, page 24; 'Word collector'

APPLY Independent writing; respond to marking

ASSESS Dictation: **I have to give you this large badge.**

Spelling 1   page 25

FOCUS Words ending with the 'ch' sound

TEACH ▶ Ask pupils to write and show: **teach, coach, church, bench**. ▶ Check spellings. Recap **ch** and long vowel spellings. ▶ Say the sounds and write on the board **catch** (**c-a-tch**). Write over the **tch** spelling in colour. ▶ Explain that the **tch** spelling is used straight after a short vowel sound (a, e, i, o, u). ▶ Revise short vowels and ask pupils to write and show **itch**. Check spellings. ▶ Explain that there are some high-frequency words that do not follow this rule (for example, **much, such, rich**) and these need to be learnt.

PRACTISE **Spelling 1**, page 25; 'Additional word list'

APPLY Spelling sentences

ASSESS Dictation: **The team march off the pitch and have lunch on the coach.**

Spelling 1   page 26

FOCUS Adding **s** or **es**

TEACH ▶ Ask pupils to write and show: **torch, pitch, coach** and **match**. ▶ Write the list of words on the board so pupils can check their spellings. ▶ Recap **tch** and **ch** endings. ▶ Add the number two before each of the words on the board. ▶ Read the new list together, orally adding the plural ending. ▶ Discuss the extra syllable that can be heard (for example, **torch/es**) and show how to add **es** to spell the words. ▶ Establish that if the ending sounds like 'iz' and adds an extra beat, add **es**. ▶ Ask pupils to add **es** to the words they have written. ▶ Demonstrate that the same thing happens with words ending **sh** (for example, write **dish/es**).

PRACTISE **Spelling 1**, page 26; 'Additional word list'; 'Word sort 1'

APPLY Independent writing; paired review; respond to marking

ASSESS Dictation: **Pack three torches and a box of matches.**

Spelling 1   page 27

FOCUS Tricky words 4

TEACH ▶ On the board, write **all**. Say the word in a sentence. ▶ Discuss what makes the word tricky and why errors are made (the **a** spelling of the 'aw' sound). ▶ Ask pupils to practise saying and writing the word a number of times to get a feel for the correct spelling. ▶ Cover it and ask pupils to write the sentence: We **all** did. Reveal the word to check the spelling. ▶ Once pupils are confident with the word **all**, ask them to use what they have learnt to write and show **ball**. Explain that the **all** spelling pattern is found in a number of words (for example, **call, tall, fall**).

PRACTISE **Spelling 1**, page 27; 'Words to practise: My tricky words'

APPLY Independent writing; respond to marking; paired review

ASSESS Dictation: **I told you to find the ball and hold it on the wall.**

Spelling 1   page 28

FOCUS The 'or' sound

TEACH ▶ Say some words with the **or** spelling for pupils to write and show (for example, **fork**, **born**, **for**). Check the spellings. ▶ Ask pupils to suggest words that rhyme with **for** (have the 'or' sound at the end). ▶ Say the sounds and write these words on the board to gather different **or** spellings at the end of words. ▶ Underline the letters that represent the 'or' sound (for example, m<u>ore</u>, s<u>aw</u>). ▶ Establish that **ore** and **aw** are the main spellings at the end of words but there are other spellings in common everyday words that need to be learnt (for example, **door**, **four**).

PRACTISE **Spelling 1**, page 28; 'Word sort' 2 or 3

APPLY Spelling sentences

ASSESS Dictation: I <u>saw</u> the <u>corn</u> on the <u>floor</u> just <u>before</u> the <u>storm</u>.

Spelling 1   page 29

FOCUS Short 'u' and short 'e' sounds

TEACH ▶ Ask pupils to be good spellers and spot your deliberate mistake. Say the sounds and write the words **mud**, **thud**, **bud** and **gud** (instead of **good**). *Note:* Regional variations affect the pronunciation of some **oo** words. ▶ Discuss why the last spelling is incorrect. Rub off **gud** and write the correct spelling (**good**). ▶ Underline the **oo** spelling and explain that this spelling of 'u' is found in a number of words. ▶ Ask pupils to write **hood**.

Repeat the same activity with the words **bed**, **shed** and **hed** (**head**). ▶ Establish that the 'e' sound is spelt **ea** in **head** and in other words.

PRACTISE **Spelling 1**, page 29; 'Word sort 1'

APPLY Spelling sentences

ASSESS Dictation: Mum <u>took</u> a <u>look</u> at my <u>foot</u> and <u>shook</u> her <u>head</u>.

Spelling 1   page 30

FOCUS Spelling words starting with **wh**

TEACH ▶ Display a list of question words: **when, which, where, why.** ▶ Read them together and discuss what else they all have in common (all start with **wh**). ▶ Explain that the **wh** sounds very like **w** so it is important to remember which words start **wh**. As there are not many **wh** words, it is easier to learn and remember them. ▶ Ask pupils if they know any other **wh** words (for example, **white, whisper**). Say the sounds and write these words on the board to start a collection of **wh** words to display in the classroom.

PRACTISE **Spelling 1**, page 30; 'Additional word list'

APPLY Spelling sentences; independent writing (for example, questions)

ASSESS Dictation: <u>Which</u> <u>wheel</u> will fit the <u>white</u> car?

Spelling 1   page 31

FOCUS Spelling words starting with **kn**

TEACH ▶ Write **knee** on the board. ▶ Say the sounds and point to the letters. Underline the **kn** spelling of the 'n' sound at the start of this word. ▶ Discuss other examples of **kn** words pupils might know from reading. ▶ Demonstrate the strategy of saying **k-n** as you say the sounds and write the words on the board (for example, **k-n-o-ck**). ▶ You could explain that hundreds of years ago the **k** was sounded, but now it is only the spelling that is retained in just a few words. ▶ Start a collection of **kn** words to be learnt.

PRACTISE **Spelling 1**, page 31; 'Word collector'

APPLY Spelling sentences; independent writing

ASSESS Dictation: The door <u>knob</u> is missing so the <u>knight</u> must <u>knock</u>.

Spelling 1 — page 32

FOCUS Adding **ed**

TEACH ▶ Say a list of verbs for pupils to write and show (for example, **play**, **look**, **hunt**, **sail**, **hiss**). ▶ Write the list on the board so pupils can check their spellings. Then go down the list orally adding **ed**, for example, say: *Yesterday I played.* ▶ Show how to add **ed** to make **play** into **played**. ▶ Repeat the procedure with **look/ed** and **hunt/ed**. Clarify that although the ending sounds like 't' in **looked** and 'id' in **hunted**, it is always spelt **ed**. ▶ Let pupils change the other words orally and in writing.

PRACTISE Spelling 1, page 32; 'Additional word list'

APPLY Set target; independent writing; paired review; respond to marking

ASSESS Dictation: **I** <u>rushed</u> and <u>helped</u> my sister get up.

Spelling 1 — page 33

FOCUS Tricky words 5

TEACH ▶ Select two words pupils frequently spell incorrectly (for example, **your**, **want**). ▶ Write one on the board and say it in a sentence (for example, *I want to help*). ▶ Say the sounds as you point to the appropriate letters in the word. ▶ Identify the tricky bit and discuss why errors are made, for example, **wont** (a is not the usual spelling for the 'o' sound). ▶ Discuss ways to remember the correct spelling, for example, link it to the word **was** or say it as it's spelt (**w-a-n-t**). Ask pupils to say this a few times as they trace the word with their finger. ▶ Cover the word and ask pupils to write: I **want** to help. Check spellings. ▶ Repeat the process with the second word.

PRACTISE Spelling 1, page 33; 'Words to practise: My tricky words'

APPLY Set mini-target; independent writing; respond to marking

ASSESS Dictation: <u>Ask</u> <u>Mr</u> and <u>Mrs</u> Green <u>what</u> they <u>want</u> for tea.

Spelling 1 — page 34

FOCUS The 'ear' sound

TEACH ▶ Ask pupils to write and show **here**. Check spellings. ▶ Ask for words that rhyme with **here**. Write the words on the board as they are suggested, so pupils can see the different spellings. ▶ Identify and underline the letters that spell the **ear** phoneme in each word. ▶ Discuss which spelling is most common (**ear**, followed by **eer**; only a few words are spelt **ere**). ▶ Clarify the difference between **hear** and **here**. Remind pupils to say *I hear with my ear* to remember the correct spelling.

PRACTISE Spelling 1, page 34; 'Word sort 2'

APPLY Spelling sentences

ASSESS Dictation: **It is** <u>clear</u> **from the** <u>cheer</u> **that the queen is now** <u>near</u>.

Spelling 1 — page 35

FOCUS The 'air' sound

TEACH ▶ Ask pupils to write and show: Up in the **air**. ▶ Discuss the spelling of **air**. Write it on the board. ▶ Ask pupils to suggest words that rhyme with **air**. Suggestions are likely to include some homophones (for example, **pair** and **pear**), so ask pupils to say their suggestions in a sentence to establish which they mean. ▶ Say the sounds and write each word on the board as it is suggested, underlining the spelling of the 'air' sound (for example, ch<u>air</u>, b<u>ear</u>, c<u>are</u>, th<u>ere</u>). ▶ Explain that they need to learn which spelling each word uses.

PRACTISE Spelling 1, page 35; 'Additional word list'

APPLY Spelling sentences

ASSESS Dictation: **The** <u>bear</u> **went** <u>upstairs</u> **to find a** <u>chair</u> **to** <u>share</u>.

Spelling 1 — page 36

FOCUS The 'k' sound

TEACH ▶ Show flashcards for **c**, **k** and **ck**. Establish that they all represent the 'k' sound. ▶ Explain that when spelling a word you need to know which one to use. ▶ Ask pupils to be good spellers and spot errors in the words you write. Say the sounds and write, for example, **stuck**, **thank**, **parck**. ▶ Discuss the mistake, recapping the **ck** spelling at the end of a word (or syllable) after a short vowel ('a', 'i', 'e', 'o', 'u'), but **k** if it follows a long vowel or is in a blend. ▶ Repeat the activity with errors at the start of words (for example, **skarf**, **scin**). ▶ Explain that a useful guideline is to use **k** before **i** or **e** and **c** in other situations.

PRACTISE Spelling 1, page 36; 'Additional word list'

APPLY Set target; independent writing

ASSESS Dictation: **Skip** **back** to the **track** in the **park**.

Spelling 1 — page 37

FOCUS Words ending with the 's' sound

TEACH ▶ Say words with **ss** endings for pupils to write and show (for example, **miss**, **cross**, **fuss**). ▶ Check spellings. Recap that **ss** follows a short vowel ('a', 'i', 'e', 'o', 'u'). ▶ Explain that if the 's' sound comes after a long vowel, it is spelt **se** or sometimes **ce**. ▶ Say the sounds in the word **horse**. Emphasise the long 'or' sound orally and by moving your hands apart. ▶ Ask pupils to say the sounds as you write the word on the board (**h-or-se**). ▶ Ask pupils to write **cheese**. ▶ Repeat with a word ending **ce** (for example, **race**).

PRACTISE Spelling 1, page 37; 'Word sort 1' (**se** and **ce** words)

APPLY Independent writing

ASSESS Dictation: **The** **mouse** in the **house** was looking for a **slice** of **cheese**.

Spelling 1 — page 38

FOCUS Two-syllable words ending with long 'e'

TEACH ▶ Say one-syllable words ending with long 'ee' sound for pupils to write and show (for example, **tree**, **he**, **knee**, **tea**). Check spellings. ▶ Say a two-syllable word ending with the 'ee' sound (for example, **party**). Clap the two syllables. ▶ Demonstrate saying the sounds and writing the first syllable (**p-ar**) and then the second (**t-y**). ▶ Explain that in two-syllable words a long 'ee' ending is spelt **y** or sometimes **ey**. ▶ Help pupils to say the syllables and write the word **body**.

PRACTISE Spelling 1, page 38; 'Additional word list'

APPLY Spelling sentences

ASSESS Dictation: **Are you** **ready** for a **story** about a **very** **silly** **donkey**?

Spelling 1 — page 39

FOCUS Tricky words 6

TEACH ▶ Identify any previously taught tricky words that pupils are still misspelling in their independent writing. ▶ Add these words to the list in the pupil book or use the 'Words to practise: My tricky words' copymaster to create individual lists. ▶ Recap the process of taking the word apart, identifying the tricky bit and finding a way to remember it. ▶ Ask pupils to explain how they might learn and remember a tricky word, for example, making links to known words (**once** looks like **one**; I can say **e-very**).

PRACTISE Spelling 1, page 39; 'Words to practise: My tricky words'

APPLY Set mini-target; independent writing

ASSESS Dictation: **There was** **once** a girl with very **long** hair. It was so **long** she **began** to trip over it.

Spelling 2

Spelling 2   page 4

FOCUS The long 'a' sound

TEACH ▶ Ask pupils to write and show: **away, rain, take.** ▶ Check spellings. Recap long 'a' spellings and familiar patterns, for example: **ay** at the end; **ai** or **a-e** in the middle; **ain, ake, ave** patterns. ▶ Say a less familiar word (for example, **stain**). Say the sounds and write **st-n**. ▶ Ask pupils to make a reasoned choice for the correct long 'a' spelling. ▶ Write in **ai** and model looking to check that it looks right. ▶ Repeat with **crane** (**cr n**). Write **crain** and **crane**. Discuss which version looks right. ▶ Explain that patterns are helpful but not all words follow them, so it is necessary to learn the correct spelling for some words.

PRACTISE Spelling 2, page 4; 'Additional word list'; 'Word sort 1'

APPLY Set target; independent writing

ASSESS Dictation: **There is no space in the shade so we have to wait for a place.**

Spelling 2   page 5

FOCUS The long 'i' sound

TEACH ▶ Ask pupils to write and show: **fright, fine, like, slide, fly.** ▶ Check spellings. Recap long 'i' spellings and patterns, for example: **igh/t** at the end; **i-e** in the middle. ▶ Explain that not all words follow these patterns. Demonstrate with the word **kite.** ▶ Reinforce that it is important to learn the correct spelling for individual words. ▶ Generate a list of words that rhyme with **fly.** Write them on the board, underlining the long 'i' spellings (for example, **fly, pie, high**). ▶ Explain that although **y** is the most common spelling at the end of words, **igh** and **ie** are other spellings and appear in some common words, which should be learnt.

PRACTISE Spelling 2, page 5; 'Additional word list'

APPLY Set target; independent writing

ASSESS Dictation: **His wife had a fright when she saw the pie on fire.**

Spelling 2   page 6

FOCUS The long 'o' sound

TEACH ▶ Ask pupils to write and show: **coat, road, joke, hose, rope.** Include one or two familiar tricky words to revise alternative spellings in a few words (for example, **no, old, most**). ▶ Say the sounds and discuss how to spell the word **goal.** If pupils suggest **gole** (like **pole, hole**), write it and ask if it looks right. ▶ Discuss alternative spellings and write **g-oa-l.** ▶ Reinforce the importance of learning the right spelling and checking to see if a spelling looks right. ▶ Repeat with **bowl, roll, toe.** Underline the long 'o' spelling in each word. ▶ Explain that **oe** is another way of spelling long 'o', found in a few words.

PRACTISE Spelling 2, page 6; 'Additional word list'

APPLY Set target; independent writing; respond to marking

ASSESS Dictation: **I hope the gold cloak is on the throne**

Spelling 2   page 7

FOCUS The long 'e' sound

TEACH ▶ Ask pupils to write and show: **keep, eat, green.** ▶ Check spellings. ▶ Say a word with two possible spellings (for example, **meal** (meel)). ▶ Ask pupils to write which they think it is and then check if it looks correct before they show it. ▶ Write the correct spelling on the board to reinforce it. ▶ Say the word **thief.** Say the sounds as you write it on the board. ▶ Underline the **ie** spelling. Explain that this is another spelling for the long 'e' sound found in a few words. ▶ Ask pupils to spell the word **chief.** ▶ Repeat with the word **these** to introduce the **e-e** spelling. Ask pupils to write **eve.**

PRACTISE Spelling 2, page 7; 'Additional word list'

APPLY Set target; independent writing; respond to marking

ASSESS Dictation: **A thief sneaks down the street to steal these wheels.**

Spelling 2 page 8

FOCUS The long 'oo' sound

TEACH ▶ Ask pupils to write and show: **blue**, **glue**; **chew**, **flew**; **moon**, **soon**. ▶ Check spellings. Recap spellings of the long 'oo' sound. ▶ Say a word with two possible spellings (for example, **June** (Joon), **rude** (rood)). Ask pupils to write which they think it is and then check to see if it looks right before showing it. ▶ Write the correct spelling on the board. ▶ Say words with a 'yoo' sound (for example, **cube**, **new**, **cue**). Say the sounds as you write the letters on the board. ▶ Establish that **u-e**, **ue** and **ew** are also the usual spellings for the 'yoo' sound.

PRACTISE Spelling 2, page 8; 'Word sort 2'

APPLY Independent writing; respond to marking

ASSESS Dictation: **I** <u>choose</u> **to** <u>use</u> **this** <u>tube</u> **of** <u>glue</u> **to fix my** <u>boots</u>.

Spelling 2 page 9

FOCUS Tricky words 1

TEACH ▶ The words on page 9 have unusual spellings of long vowel phonemes. ▶ Select a word that pupils often spell incorrectly and write it on the board (for example, **great**). ▶ Demonstrate how to take the word apart by saying the sounds and writing the corresponding letters (**g-r-ea-t**). Underline the tricky part (**ea**). ▶ Discuss a memory strategy (for example, *look for the word eat*). Let pupils use this strategy to practise writing the word a few times. ▶ Cover the word and ask pupils to write: It is **great** to **eat**.

PRACTISE Spelling 2, page 9; 'Words to practise: My tricky words'

APPLY Set mini-targets; independent writing; respond to marking

ASSESS Dictation: **The** <u>lady</u> **had a** <u>great</u> **time when she went to** <u>buy</u> **new** <u>shoes</u>.

Spelling 2 page 10

FOCUS Adding **ing**

TEACH ▶ Write a verb on the board (for example, **stamp**). ▶ Mime the action together. Say: *We are stamping.* ▶ Write the verb with the extra syllable **ing** added. ▶ Repeat with other words. Include some root words ending with **e** (for example, **ride** (**riding**), **wave** (**waving**)). ▶ Look at the lists of verbs. Discuss the pattern. ▶ Establish that when a word ends with **e**, the **e** is dropped when **ing** is added. ▶ Discuss other examples (for example, **hope** (**hoping**)). ▶ Model writing the root word but dropping the **e** before adding **ing**.

PRACTISE Spelling 2, page 10; 'Additional word list'

APPLY Set target; independent writing

ASSESS Dictation: **The pupils were** <u>cheering</u>, <u>smiling</u> **and** <u>waving</u>.

Spelling 2 page 11

FOCUS Adding **ed**

TEACH ▶ Ask pupils to write and show: **falling**, **jumping**, **hoping**. Recap verbs and adding **ing**. ▶ Practise orally changing verb tense. ▶ Write a verb on the board (for example, **jump**). Say: *Today I am **jumping**. Yesterday I jumped.* Write **jumped** on the board. ▶ Repeat with other words. Include some verbs ending with **e** (for example, **bake**). ▶ Look at the past tense verbs. ▶ Explain that even though the final phoneme sometimes sounds like 'id' or 't', it is always spelt **ed** (for example, **started**, **jumped**). ▶ Discuss the pattern for words ending with **e**. Establish that the **e** is dropped when **ed** is added. ▶ Give other examples. Ask pupils to add **ed**.

PRACTISE Spelling 2, page 11; 'Additional word list'

APPLY Set target; independent writing; respond to marking

ASSESS Dictation: **The boys** <u>shouted</u> **and** <u>waved</u> **as they** <u>dived</u> **into the pool.**

Spelling 2   page 12

FOCUS Doubling letters before **ing** and **ed**

TEACH ▶ Repeat the tense-changing activity described above. This time include some words that require consonants to be doubled (for example, **hum**) and some that do not (for example, **dream**). ▶ Look at the past tense verbs. ▶ Discuss the pattern. Explain that the last letter is doubled if a root word ends with a short vowel sound ('a', 'e', 'i', 'o', 'u') and a single letter. ▶ (Another way to explain this is that there must be two consonants between a short vowel and the **ed** to keep the short vowel short.) ▶ Show that the same rule applies to add **ing** (for example, **humming**).

PRACTISE **Spelling** 2, page 12; 'Additional word list'; 'Word sort 1'

APPLY Independent writing; respond to marking

ASSESS Dictation: **They hopped and skipped along as the dog barked and wagged his tail.**

Spelling 2   page 13

FOCUS Adding **ing** and **ed** to words ending **y**

TEACH ▶ Ask pupils to write and show: **begged**, **liked**, **ruled**. ▶ Check spellings. Recap rules for adding **ed** (for example: drop **e**; double consonants). ▶ Write the word **fry**. Say: *Today I fry eggs. Yesterday I fried eggs.* Write **fried** on the board. ▶ Repeat with the word **try** (**tried**). ▶ Look at the past tense verbs. ▶ Discuss the pattern. Explain that if a word ends consonant **y**, the **y** is changed to an **i** before **ed** is added. ▶ Ask pupils to write **cry** and **cried**. ▶ Now say: *I am frying...* and write **frying** on the board. ▶ Explain that no change is needed to add **ing** (because that would make a double **i**). ▶ Ask pupils to write **crying**.

PRACTISE **Spelling** 2, page 13; 'Word sort 1'

APPLY Independent writing; respond to marking

ASSESS Dictation: **He cried and cried but Mum dried his tears.**

Spelling 2   page 14

FOCUS Revision 1

TEACH ▶ Reinforce rules for adding **ing** and **ed**. ▶ Focus on the rule that pupils are having difficulty applying in their independent writing. ▶ Remind them to refer to the relevant pages in **Spelling** 2 to help them when writing. ▶ Write a sentence on the board to demonstrate proof reading, checking for spelling errors associated with **ing** or **ed** endings. ▶ Encourage pupils to be good spellers and find the mistakes. ▶ Discuss the correct spelling and reinforce the rule that will avoid the same error in the future (for example: drop **e**; change **y** to **i**; double the consonant after a short vowel).

PRACTISE **Spelling** 2, page 14

APPLY Proof reading; respond to marking

ASSESS Through independent writing

Spelling 2   page 15

FOCUS Tricky words 2

TEACH ▶ The words on page 15 have unusual spellings of the 'u' sound. (Regional variations affect pronunciation of some of the words.) ▶ Select a word pupils have difficulty with (for example, **other**, **could**). Write it on the board. ▶ Demonstrate taking the word apart, saying the sounds and writing the corresponding letters. ▶ Underline the 'u' spelling that causes problems (for example, o-th-er; c-**oul**-d). ▶ Ask pupils to finger trace or write the word, saying o-ther, or chanting letter names (o-u-l). ▶ Cover the word and ask pupils to write it. ▶ Explain that other words follow the same spelling patterns. ▶ Ask them to write **mother** and **brother** or **would** and **should**.

PRACTISE **Spelling** 2, page 15; 'Words to practise: My tricky words'

APPLY Set mini-target; independent writing; proof reading; respond to marking

ASSESS Dictation: **My brother would have done nothing.**

Spelling 2   page 16

FOCUS Adding **s** and **es**

TEACH ▶ Practise forming plurals. Ask pupils to write and show: **One tent, two tents. One cake, two cakes**. Check. ▶ Say some nouns ending with hissing and buzzing sounds ('sh', 'ch', 'x', 'zz', 'ss'), for example, **dish, church, box**. ▶ Draw attention to the change in the sound as these words are made into plurals (an extra syllable is added with an 'iz' sound, for example, **dish-es**). ▶ Recap that **es** is added when this sound is heard. ▶ Explain that the extra syllable makes the **s** ending easier to say after hissing and buzzing sounds. ▶ Write **boxes, dishes, churches**.

PRACTISE Spelling 2, page 16; 'Additional word list'

APPLY Set target; independent writing

ASSESS Dictation: **The buses, bikes, coaches and trucks stopped at the lights.**

Spelling 2   page 17

FOCUS Adding **s** to words ending **y**

TEACH ▶ Ask pupils to write and show a shopping list: **crisps, sweets, grapes, cakes, matches**. ▶ Check spellings. Recap rules for adding **s** or **es**. ▶ Write on the board some items ending with **y**: **jelly, lolly, turkey**. ▶ Go down the list orally changing the words into plurals and changing the words on the board accordingly (**jellies, lollies, turkeys**). ▶ Discuss the pattern. Establish that if a word ends consonant **y**, change the **y** to **i** and then add **es**. But if the word ends with a vowel and a **y**, just add **s**.

PRACTISE Spelling 2, page 17; 'Additional word list'

APPLY Set target; independent writing

ASSESS Dictation: **Did the monkeys drop jellies on the ladies?**

Spelling 2   page 18

FOCUS The **w** special

TEACH ▶ Ask pupils to write the words **was** and **want**. ▶ Write the words on the board so pupils can check their spellings. ▶ Underline the tricky part (the 'wo' sound is spelt **wa**). Explain that many **w** words follow this pattern. ▶ Ask pupils to use this knowledge to write and show **wash**.

Discuss how to spell **word**. ▶ Say the sounds and write it on the board. ▶ Underline the **wor** spelling. Explain that **w** followed by an 'ur' sound is sometimes spelt **wor** (but not in the word **were**). ▶ Ask pupils to write **work**.

PRACTISE Spelling 2, page 18; 'Word collector'

APPLY Spelling sentences; proof read; respond to marking

ASSESS Dictation: **The wasps were watching the man working near the swamp.**

Spelling 2   page 19

FOCUS The **q** special

TEACH ▶ Say the sounds and write the word **queen**. ▶ Establish that the sound 'kw' is spelt **qu**. ▶ Explain that **q** is always followed by **u**. (A useful mnemonic is: *The queen always has an umbrella*). ▶ Ask pupils to write and show **quake**.

Sound spell and write the word **square** (s/qu/are). Establish that the sound 's/kw' is spelt **s/qu**. ▶ Repeat with the word **squash** (s/qu/a/sh). Explain that the special **w** rule they have just learnt also applies to words with the 'k/w' or 'sk/w' sound.

PRACTISE Spelling 2, page 19; 'Word collector'

APPLY Spelling sentences

ASSESS Dictation: **The queen squeals as the room quivers and quakes.**

Spelling 2 page 20

FOCUS Soft **g**

TEACH ► Ask pupils to write and show: **large**, **stage**, **bridge**. ► Check spellings. Recap that a 'j' sound at the end of a word is always spelt **ge** (or **dge** after a short vowel). ► Say the word **village**. Demonstrate saying the syllables (**vill/age**) and writing **v-i-ll** and **age**. ► Explain that in two syllable words the 'ij' ending is spelt **age**. ► Ask pupils to write **cottage**.

Say the sounds and write the words **giant** and **magic**. Explain that the **g** spelling of a 'j' sound is also found at the start or in the middle of some words. ► Explain that a 'j' sound is often spelt **g** before **i**, **e** or **y**.

PRACTISE **Spelling 2**, page 20; 'Word collector'

APPLY Spelling sentences

ASSESS Dictation: **The <u>strange</u> <u>ginger</u> cat stopped at the <u>edge</u> of the <u>village</u>.**

Spelling 2 page 21

FOCUS Tricky words 3

TEACH ► Select a word that pupils are misspelling (for example, **walk**). Write it on the board. ► Demonstrate taking the word apart by saying the sounds and writing the corresponding letters. ► Write over the tricky part in colour (**w-<u>al</u>-k**) and discuss why it is often misspelt (an unusual spelling of the 'aw' sound). ► Make a link to the words **all**, **wall** etc. which share the same spelling pattern. Discuss using this to help remember the correct spelling for **walk** (for example, *like* **wall** *but with a k*). ► Let pupils practise saying this while writing or finger tracing the word a few times. ► Cover the word and ask pupils to write: I **walk** fast.

PRACTISE **Spelling 2**, page 21; 'Words to practise: My tricky words'

APPLY Set mini-target; independent writing; respond to marking

ASSESS Dictation: **<u>Anyway</u>, it was my <u>father</u> <u>who</u> had the last <u>laugh</u>.**

Spelling 2 page 22

FOCUS Adding the suffix **y**

TEACH ► On the board write **Mr Happy**. Recap the **y** spelling of long 'e' at the end of two-syllable words. ► Explain that **y** is a suffix that can be added to words to make describing words. ► Sound spell and write the word **greed**. Say **Mr Greedy** and add the **y** suffix. ► Repeat with other words (for example, **gloom**, **boss**, **cheek**). ► Write the word **laze**. ► Recap the drop the **e** rule for adding **ing**. ► Explain that **e** is also dropped when the **y** suffix is added. Demonstrate changing **laze** to **lazy**. ► Write the word **flop**. ► Recap the double the last letter rule for adding **ed/ing**.► Explain that this also applies when **y** is added. Demonstrate changing **flop** to **floppy**.

PRACTISE **Spelling 2**, page 22; 'Additional word list'; 'Word sort 1'

APPLY Set target; independent writing (for example, description) or spelling sentences

ASSESS Dictation: **It was <u>gloomy</u> and <u>scary</u> inside the old <u>spooky</u> house.**

Spelling 2 page 23

FOCUS Adding **er** and **est**

TEACH ► Introduce comparative suffixes through discussion of story characters, for example: *Monkey was fast*; *hare was faster*; *but cheetah was fastest*. ► Write the adjectives on the board. ► Write over **er** and **est** suffixes in colour. ► Explain that **er** means more and **est** means most. ► Ask pupils to write **slow**, **slower**, **slowest**. Repeat with a word ending with **e** (for example, **brave**, **braver**, **bravest**) and a word that requires the consonant to be doubled (for example, **big**, **bigger**, **biggest**). ► Establish that these are the same rules as when adding **ed**, **ing** and **y**. ► Ask pupils to write **fatter** and **nicer**.

PRACTISE **Spelling 2**, page 23; 'Additional word list'

APPLY Add to target; independent writing or spelling sentences

ASSESS Dictation: **He was the <u>biggest</u>, <u>fattest</u>, <u>widest</u> and <u>kindest</u> pig in the farmyard.**

Spelling 2   page 24

FOCUS Adding **ful** and **less**

TEACH ▶ On the board write **helpful**. Discuss what it means to be helpful. ▶ Explain that **ful** is another suffix used to form describing words. ▶ Ensure that pupils understand that the suffix is spelt **ful** not **full**. ▶ Ask pupils to say the sounds as you write the word **pain**, then add **ful**. ▶ Ask pupils to read the word and use it in a sentence. ▶ Repeat with a word ending with **e** (for example, **hope**). Explain that when adding **ful** there is no need to drop the last letter. ▶ Use the words on the board to show how to change the suffix **ful** to **less** to form **painless** and **hopeless**. ▶ Reinforce that again there is no need to drop the **e**.

PRACTISE Spelling 2, page 24; 'Additional word list'

APPLY Independent writing (for example, story) or spelling sentences

ASSESS Dictation: **Anna felt <u>hopeful</u> and <u>fearless</u> as she set off.**

Spelling 2   page 25

FOCUS Words that sound the same

TEACH ▶ Dictate a short sentence for pupils to write (for example, *I can see the sea*). ▶ Discuss the different meanings and spellings of **see** and **sea**. ▶ Explain that there are many words that sound the same but have different meanings and spellings. ▶ Ask pupils for other examples, putting them into sentences to clarify meanings. ▶ Write them on the board. (It is often the spelling of the vowel phoneme that changes, so use this opportunity to reinforce the different spellings.) ▶ Explain that it is important to know the meaning of these words in order to use the right spelling on each occasion.

PRACTISE Spelling 2, page 25; 'Additional word list'

APPLY Spelling sentences; independent writing

ASSESS Dictation: **The wind <u>blew</u> the sailboat onto the <u>tail</u> of the <u>whale</u>.**

Spelling 2   page 26

FOCUS Revision 2

TEACH ▶ Reinforce rules for adding suffixes. Focus on a suffix or rule that pupils are having difficulty with in their independent writing (for example: adding **ed**; adding **y** to words ending in **e**). ▶ Write a sentence on the board or display a short piece of text with typical errors to show how to proof read, checking for spelling errors associated with adding suffixes. ▶ Ask pupils to be good spellers and find and correct the errors. ▶ Reinforce the rule that will avoid the same error in the future.

PRACTISE Spelling 2, page 26; previous 'Additional word lists'

APPLY Proof read; respond to marking; check targets

ASSESS Through independent writing

Spelling 2   page 27

FOCUS Topic words 1

TEACH ▶ Choose words from pupils' independent story writing. Select a word and write it on the board (for example, **princess**). ▶ Demonstrate taking the word apart by saying the two syllables and saying the sounds in each syllable as you write the corresponding letters. ▶ Ask pupils to say which are the easy bits (spelt as they sound) and which is the tricky part (for example, soft **c** in **cess**). ▶ Ask pupils to practise writing the word as they say it. ▶ Cover the word and ask pupils to write, for example: The **princess** was sad.

PRACTISE Spelling 2, page 27; 'Words to practise: My topic words'

APPLY Set mini-target; independent writing; respond to marking

ASSESS Dictation: **The <u>wizard</u> cast a spell and the <u>pretty</u> <u>princess</u> turned into a <u>purple</u> cat.**

Spelling 2   page 28

FOCUS Adding the prefix **un**

TEACH ► Prepare a list of words (for example, **happy, lucky, fair**). ► Use **happy** in a sentence, for example: *I feel happy when… .* ► Then add **un** and say a sentence using **unhappy**. ► Repeat with the other words, asking pupils to suggest sentences. ► Discuss how adding **un** changes the meaning of the word. Explain that **un** is a prefix; it changes the meaning but not the spelling of a word. ► Ask pupils to write and show **lucky** and then to write and show the opposite. ► Establish the spelling routine of *Write the prefix and then the word.*

PRACTISE Spelling 2, page 28; 'Additional word list'

APPLY Independent writing or spelling sentences

ASSESS Dictation: **It is <u>unlucky</u> to <u>uncover</u> the box and <u>untie</u> the string.**

Spelling 2   page 29

FOCUS Adding the prefixes **un** and **dis**

TEACH ► Display a list of words (for example, **like, agree, trust**). ► Hold a card with the prefix **dis** in front of each word and together read the new words. ► Discuss how the prefix **dis** changes the meaning of a word. Establish that **dis** is a prefix; it changes the meaning but not the spelling of a word. ► Write words on the board (for example, **unknown, appear**). ► Ask pupils to write and show words meaning the opposite by adding or removing **un** or **dis**. ► Check correct spelling of the root words and prefixes (**dis** not **diss**).

PRACTISE Spelling 2, page 29; 'Word collector'; 'Spelling log'

APPLY Independent writing (for example, story) or spelling sentences

ASSESS Dictation: **The <u>dishonest</u> wizard will <u>disappear</u> in a puff of smoke.**

Spelling 2   page 30

FOCUS Tricky consonants 1

TEACH ► Display name badges **Philip**, **Sophie** and **Ph(o)ebe**. Read the names. ► Discuss the **ph** spelling of the 'f' sound in these names. ► Explain that this spelling of 'f' is not found in everyday words, but some words do use the **ph** spelling and it is important to know and remember them. ► Ask if pupils know any (for example, **phone, photo**). ► Sound spell and write these words on the board. Underline the **ph**.

Repeat the exercise with names **Chris**, **Michael** and **Chloe** to introduce the **ch** spelling of the 'k' sound. ► Again, this spelling is not found in many short everyday words, but is in **school**.

PRACTISE Spelling 2, page 3; 'Word collector'

APPLY Spelling sentences

ASSESS Dictation: **This <u>photo</u> shows me singing the <u>chorus</u> of a song at <u>school</u>.**

Spelling 2   page 31

FOCUS Tricky consonants 2

TEACH ► Ask pupils to write and show familiar **kn** words: **knee, knock, know**. ► Check spellings. Recap silent or unspoken letters. ► Say: *I write a letter.* ► Say the sounds as you write the word **write** on the board. Write over **wr** in colour. ► Ask pupils if they know any other words starting with the **wr** spelling of the 'r' sound (for example, **wrist**). Write these on the board. ► Repeat with the word **thumb** to identify the **mb** spelling of the 'm' sound. ► Explain that there are only a few words with **wr** and **mb** spellings but they need to be learnt. ► Demonstrate the strategy of *say it as it's spelt*, sounding the silent letter (for example, **th-u-m-b**).

PRACTISE Spelling 2, page 31; 'Word collector'

APPLY Spelling sentences

ASSESS Dictation: **The <u>knight</u> <u>knocked</u> his <u>wrist</u> and made it quite <u>numb</u>.**

Spelling 2   page 32

FOCUS Soft **c**

TEACH ▶ Ask pupils to write and show: **race**, **nice**, **dance**. ▶ Check spellings. Recap that a 's' sound at the end of a word is sometimes spelt **ce**. ▶ Ask pupils to write **chance** and **prince**.

Say the sounds and write on the board the words **city** and **pencil** to illustrate that the 's' sound is sometimes spelt **c** at the start or in the middle of a word. ▶ Explain that this is usually before **i**, **e** or **y**.

PRACTISE Spelling 2, page 32; 'Word collector'

APPLY Spelling sentences

ASSESS Dictation: **The <u>prince</u> found ten <u>pence</u> in the <u>city</u> <u>centre</u>. <u>Fancy</u> that!**

Spelling 2   page 33

FOCUS Topic words 2

TEACH ▶ Ask pupils to join in with saying the days of the week and clapping the syllables. ▶ Discuss which have two syllables and which three. ▶ Demonstrate spelling the word **Wednesday** by clapping the syllables and then saying the sounds and writing each syllable (**Wed/nes/day**). ▶ Discuss how saying the syllables like this helps to spell the word. ▶ Ask pupils to use this technique to write **Wednesday**. ▶ Let pupils choose another day to practise and learn.

PRACTISE Spelling 2, page 33; 'Words to practise: My topic words'

APPLY Set mini-target; independent writing

ASSESS Dictation: **This month football training will be for an hour on <u>Thursday</u>, <u>Saturday</u> and <u>Sunday</u>.**

Spelling 2   page 34

FOCUS Two-syllable words

TEACH ▶ Say the word **market**. ▶ Recap the strategy for spelling two-syllable words: say the syllables, say the sounds and write the first syllable (**m-ar**), then the second (**k-e-t**); check the word. ▶ Remind pupils that it is important to stress or say the second syllable clearly to spell it correctly (for example, **ket** not **kit**). ▶ Say some words for pupils to write and show (for example, **flower**, **garden**, **curtain**). In each case say the second syllable clearly so they become familiar with the sounds and the correct spelling for common endings.

PRACTISE Spelling 2, page 34; 'Additional word list'

APPLY Set target; independent writing

ASSESS Dictation: **<u>Behind</u> the <u>curtain</u> I saw the <u>shadow</u> of a <u>monster</u>.**

Spelling 2   page 35

FOCUS Words ending 'shun' and 'ul'

TEACH ▶ Ask pupils to write the word **little**. ▶ Say the sounds and write it on the board so they can check their spelling. ▶ In colour, write over the **le** ending. Explain that the 'ul' ending is most often spelt **le** (although it can sometimes be spelt **el** or **al**). ▶ Ask pupils to write and show **handle**.

Say the word **fiction**. ▶ Say each syllable and write it on the board. ▶ Write over the **tion** ending in colour. Explain that the ending that sounds like 'shun' is most often spelt **tion**. ▶ Ask pupils to write **fraction**. ▶ Establish that **le** and **tion** endings are not spelt as they sound so they need to be learnt.

PRACTISE Spelling 2, page 35; 'Word collector'

APPLY Spelling sentences

ASSESS Dictation: **Mr <u>Tickle</u> and Mr <u>Little</u> went to the railway <u>station</u>.**

Spelling 2   page 36

FOCUS Taking words apart

TEACH ▶ Discuss strategies for spelling a longer word: saying the syllables or splitting it into word parts (for example, compound words into two simple words, or words with affixes into root words and prefix or suffix). ▶ Say a word (for example, **unkindness**) and demonstrate taking the word apart. ▶ Explain your thinking as you say and spell each part of the word in turn: **un-kind-ness**. ▶ Ask pupils to write and show **unwanted**. Invite them to explain the strategies they used.

PRACTISE Spelling 2, page 36; 'Spelling log'

APPLY Independent writing

ASSESS Dictation: <u>Yesterday</u>, <u>grandmother</u> made a <u>wonderful</u> <u>discovery</u> in the <u>garden</u>.

Spelling 2   page 37

FOCUS Shortened forms

TEACH ▶ Practise orally using contractions, for example, say: *Do not stop. It is not fair*. Ask pupils to provide the more natural contraction (***Don't** stop. **It's** not fair*). ▶ Use magnetic letters to build the words **do not**. ▶ Push the two words together and then take out the **o**, replacing it with an apostrophe. ▶ Read the resulting contraction. ▶ Explain that the apostrophe shows where the missing letter was (not where the two words are joined). ▶ Repeat with **it is – it's** and **has not – hasn't**. Ask pupils to write the shortened forms.

PRACTISE Spelling 2, page 37; 'Word collector'

APPLY Independent writing (for example, story with dialogue, play script)

ASSESS Dictation: <u>That's</u> not fair. I <u>can't</u> help it.

Spelling 2   page 38

FOCUS Revision 3

TEACH ▶ Revise the alternative ways of spelling sounds that have been introduced in Book 2. ▶ Focus on those which pupils are having difficulty with in their own independent writing (for example: **kn**, **wr**; soft **g** or soft **c**; or special **w**). ▶ On the board write a sentence or display a short piece of text with some typical errors. ▶ Ask pupils to be good spellers and check as you read it. ▶ Discuss alternative spellings for misspelt words that they spot, reinforcing the new spelling patterns.

PRACTISE Spelling 2, page 38

APPLY Check targets; respond to marking

ASSESS Through independent writing

Spelling 2   page 39

FOCUS Tricky words 4

TEACH ▶ Choose a word currently causing problems in independent writing (for example, **because**). ▶ Write it on the board. Invite pupils to explain how they might learn to spell it. ▶ Check that the main points are covered, for example: take the word apart, find the tricky part, decide on a way to remember it. ▶ Demonstrate this, identifying easy bits and the tricky part (**be-c-<u>au</u>-se**). ▶ Discuss a memory strategy to learn the tricky part, for example, a mnemonic (**<u>a</u>lways <u>u</u>se <u>s</u>omething <u>e</u>xtra**) or saying letter names (**a-u-s-e**) as you write it. Ask pupils to use the strategy to learn the word.

PRACTISE Spelling 2, page 39; 'Words to practise: My tricky words'

APPLY Set mini-target; independent writing; respond to marking

ASSESS Dictation: <u>Finally</u>, just <u>before</u> midnight, her new <u>clothes</u> were <u>ready</u>.

Spelling 3

Spelling 3   page 4

FOCUS Words ending **le**

TEACH ▶ Say words for pupils to write: **candle**, **tickle**, **simple**. ▶ Write the words on the board so pupils can check their spellings. ▶ Recap that **le** is the most common spelling for a final 'ul' sound. ▶ Continue to write more words (for example, **tingle**, **tremble**). ▶ Ask pupils to look for patterns in letters that commonly precede **le** endings, for example, they are often an ascender or descender (**dle**, **ble**, **kle**; **gle**, **ple**). ▶ Write over these in colour. Explain that this gives a visual cue for checking if the spelling looks right.

PRACTISE Spelling 3, page 4; 'Additional word list'

APPLY Set target (for example, spelling word endings); independent writing

ASSESS Dictation: **There was a <u>scramble</u> in the <u>jungle</u> at the first <u>rumble</u> of thunder.**

Spelling 3   page 5

FOCUS Double letters before **le**

TEACH ▶ Say words for pupils to write: **little**, **title**, **beetle**, **kettle**. ▶ Write each word on the board so pupils can check spellings. ▶ Discuss why **little** and **kettle** have double **t** and **title** and **beetle** a single **t**. ▶ If necessary, prompt pupils to listen to the preceding vowel. Establish that a short vowel sound is followed by double consonant; a long vowel is followed by a single consonant. ▶ Refer back to the **le** words on **Spelling 3**, page 4. Explain that they also had short vowels but those words already had two *different* consonants before the **le** so they did not need a double letter (for example, **tre<u>m</u>ble**, **ti<u>n</u>gle**).

PRACTISE Spelling 3, page 5; 'Additional word list'

APPLY Independent writing or spelling sentences

ASSESS Dictation: **The <u>beetle</u> floated on a <u>bubble</u> in the <u>middle</u> of a <u>puddle</u>.**

Spelling 3   page 6

FOCUS Double letters before other endings

TEACH ▶ Ask pupils to write and show: **sizzle**, **giggle**, **scramble**, **needle**, **marble**. ▶ Check spellings. Recap **le** patterns (long vowel, one consonant; short vowel, two). ▶ Explain that the same rule applies to two-syllable words with other familiar endings. ▶ Write on the board **hoping**, **hopping** and **super**, **supper**. ▶ Establish that again the double letter follows the short vowel. ▶ Ask pupils to write and show: **bitter**, **biter** and **tapping**, **taping**. ▶ Explain that some letters are never doubled (for example, **h**, **j**, **q**, **v**, **w**, **x**, as in **seven** and **boxer**).

PRACTISE Spelling 3, page 6; 'Additional word list'

APPLY Independent writing; paired review

ASSESS Dictation: **The <u>robber</u> had <u>hidden</u> his <u>supper</u> in a <u>hollow</u> tree at the <u>bottom</u> of the garden.**

Spelling 3   page 7

FOCUS Words ending **el**, **al** and **il**

TEACH ▶ Ask pupils to write and show: **simple**, **cuddle**, **table**, **chuckle**. ▶ Check spellings. Recap **le** spelling patterns (for example, often preceded by ascender or descender: **dle**, **ble**, **ple**). ▶ Explain that **le** is the most common 'ul' ending, but some words have 'ul' endings spelt **el** or **al** or even **il**. (Depending on pronunciation, the **il** ending is sometimes distinguishable by sound.)

Sound spell and write: **camel**, **metal**, **April**. ▶ Write over the endings in colour. Demonstrate how exaggerating the pronunciation of the second syllable can help to remember these spellings. ▶ Explain that visual cues (the shape of the word and whether it looks right) are also useful for distinguishing **el** from **le**, as **el** tends to follow short consonants (for example, **n**, **s**, **v**, **w**).

PRACTISE Spelling 3, page 7; 'Additional word list'

APPLY Spelling sentences

ASSESS Dictation: **The <u>pupil</u> wrote a <u>label</u> for his <u>model</u> of a <u>tunnel</u>.**

Spelling 3   page 8

FOCUS More word endings

TEACH ▶ Ask pupils to write and show **curtain** and **target**. ▶ Check spellings. Recap stressing the second syllable to help spell unstressed **ain** and **et** endings (for example, cur<u>tain</u> not cur<u>tin</u>). ▶ Ask pupils to write and show **village** and **fiction**. ▶ Check spellings. Recap that **age** and **tion** endings are not spelt as they sound, so it is important to recognise them and know the correct spelling. ▶ Say the word **present**. Write the first syllable, **pre**. ▶ Discuss how to spell the second syllable. Write in **sent**. ▶ Repeat with **distant**. ▶ Explain that some endings sound the same but are spelt differently. Stressing the difference is a useful strategy (for example, **pre/<u>sent</u>**, **dis/<u>tant</u>**)

PRACTISE **Spelling 3**, page 8; 'Spelling log'

APPLY Check targets; independent writing; respond to marking

ASSESS Dictation: **The <u>captain</u> sent an <u>important</u> <u>message</u> from the <u>distant</u> <u>planet</u>.**

Spelling 3   page 9

FOCUS Topic words 1

TEACH ▶ Show a poster or calendar with the months of the year. ▶ Practise saying the months in syllables, clapping and counting syllables. ▶ Discuss which are easy to spell (for example, **March** and **May**). ▶ Demonstrate how saying the syllables helps spell others (for example, **Sep/tem/ber**). ▶ Say and write the syllables of a tricky word (for example, **Feb ru a ry**). ▶ Identify the tricky part (for example, unstressed **r** in the second syllable). Explain that saying it as it's spelt (**Feb-ru-a-ry**) is a useful strategy for remembering it. ▶ Help pupils use this strategy to practise writing the word.

PRACTISE **Spelling 3**, page 9; 'Words to practise: My topic words'

APPLY Set mini-target; independent writing

ASSESS Dictation: **The winter months are <u>November</u>, <u>December</u>, <u>January</u> and <u>February</u>.**

Spelling 3   page 10

FOCUS Adding **ed**

TEACH ▶ Say action sentences in the present tense (for example: *I moan and groan*; *I hop and flop*; *I dance and prance*; *I wiggle and giggle*) and ask pupils to change them orally to the past tense. ▶ Ask pupils to write and show the present tense and the past tense of the verbs. ▶ Check spellings, writing the verbs on the board. ▶ Revise the rules for adding **ed**: 1. Just add **ed** (even if it sounds like 'id' or 't'); 2. Drop the final **e**; 3. Double the final consonant if there is a short vowel and a single consonant (i.e. there must be two letters between the vowel and the **ed** to keep the vowel sound short).

PRACTISE **Spelling 3**, page 10; 'Additional word list'

APPLY Set target; independent writing; respond to marking

ASSESS Dictation: **I was so <u>amazed</u> when I <u>stepped</u> inside. I just <u>stopped</u> and <u>stared</u>.**

Spelling 3   page 11

FOCUS Adding **ed** and **ing** to words ending **y**

TEACH ▶ Say the sentence *I hurry and scurry*. ▶ Say the sounds and write on the board **hurry and scurry**. ▶ Recap the **y** spelling for long 'e' at the end of two-syllable words. ▶ Orally change the sentence into the past tense. ▶ Write on the board the words **hurried** and **scurried**. ▶ Discuss the change in spelling when the **ed** is added (**y** changes to **i**). ▶ Repeat with the sentence *I stay and play*. ▶ Establish that the change **y** to an **i** rule only applies to words ending with consonant **y**.

PRACTISE **Spelling 3**, page 11; 'Word sort 1'

APPLY Independent writing; proof reading; respond to marking

ASSESS Dictation: **The cat <u>looked</u> <u>worried</u> as the mice <u>hurried</u> and <u>scurried</u> everywhere.**

Spelling 3   page 12

FOCUS Irregular past tense

TEACH ▶ Ask pupils to write and show: **bullied**, **walked**, **raced**, **slipped**. ▶ Check spelling. Recap adding **ed** to form past tense verbs. ▶ Say: *I throwed the ball. I taked it home.* Ask whether this sounds right. ▶ Explain that not all verbs add **ed** to change tense. Say the sounds and write on the board **throw** and then **threw**; **take** and then **took**. ▶ Discuss how the words change (the vowel sound changes). ▶ Say more pairs of words that follow a similar pattern (for example, **grow/grew**, **shake/shook**). Ask pupils to write and show them. ▶ Introduce a word that changes more than the vowel sound (for example, **think/ thought**). Discuss a strategy for remembering this tricky spelling.

PRACTISE **Spelling 3**, page 12; 'Additional word list'

APPLY Add to target; independent writing; respond to marking

ASSESS Dictation: **When I <u>found</u> he <u>wore</u> the stolen ring I <u>knew</u> I had <u>caught</u> the real thief.**

Spelling 3   page 13

FOCUS Adding **s** and **es**

TEACH ▶ Ask pupils to write and show a list of story characters (for example, **lady**, **donkey**, **fairy**, **witch**, **prince**, **princess**). ▶ Check spellings. ▶ Ask pupils to add **s** or **es** to change the words into plurals. ▶ Check spellings. Recap rules for adding **s** or **es** (just add **s**; add **es** after hissing or buzzing sounds/when you can hear the extra 'iz' syllable; change the **y** to **i** and add **es** if a word ends consonant **y**).

Say sentences, for example: *The witch **crashes** her broomstick. The lady **empties** the bucket.* ▶ Demonstrate writing the verbs on the board. Establish that the same rules apply when adding **s** or **es** to these words.

PRACTISE **Spelling 3**, page 13; 'Additional word list'

APPLY Set target; independent writing

ASSESS Dictation: **Jack <u>replies</u> that he has no <u>worries</u> about <u>bullies</u>.**

Spelling 3   page 14

FOCUS Revision 1

TEACH ▶ Use this session to reinforce rules for adding **ed**, **ing** and **s**. ▶ Focus on whichever pupils are having difficulty with in their independent writing. ▶ Use two or three prepared sentences to proof read together. ▶ Ask pupils to check for spelling errors associated with these endings. ▶ Reinforce the rule or knowledge that will avoid the same error in the future (for example: drop **e**; double the consonant; change **y** to **i**; irregular verbs).

PRACTISE **Spelling 3**, page 14; previous 'Additional word lists'; 'Word sort' 2 or 3

APPLY Proof reading; respond to marking; check targets

ASSESS Through independent writing

Spelling 3   page 15

FOCUS Topic words 2

TEACH ▶ Select one or two words relevant to your current maths work and write them on the board (for example, **height**, **minute**). ▶ Demonstrate taking the word apart by saying the sounds (or syllables and then sounds) as you write the corresponding letters. ▶ Identify easy bits and the tricky part (**h-<u>eigh</u>-t**, **min/<u>ute</u>**). ▶ Decide on a memory strategy, for example, relating **height** to **eight** or saying it as it's spelt: **min-ute**. ▶ Ask pupils to practise using the strategy to write the word a few times. ▶ Cover the word to see if they remember it.

PRACTISE **Spelling 3**, page 15; 'Words to practise: My topic words'

APPLY Set mini-target; independent writing

ASSESS Dictation: **It will take a <u>minute</u> to find the <u>height</u> and <u>weight</u> of a <u>cylinder</u>.**

Spelling 3 page 16

FOCUS Spelling patterns: **c** and **k**

TEACH ▶ Ask pupils to write and show: **track, thank, ticket, sparkle**. ▶ Check spellings. Recap guidelines for spelling the 'k' sound at the end of short words and syllables (**ck** after a short vowel; **k** after a long vowel or consonant). ▶ Say and write: **magic, comic, topic**. Establish that at the end of two-syllable words like these the 'k' sound is spelt **c**. ▶ In colour, write over the **ic** endings.

Write s_etch (sketch), s_ittle (skittle), s_ab (scab). ▶ Discuss clues for when to use **k** and **c**. Establish that **k** is more likely before **e, i** and **y**; **c** before other letters.

PRACTISE Spelling 3, page 16; 'Additional word list'

APPLY Spelling sentences; independent writing

ASSESS Dictation: **I packed a fantastic picnic in my plastic rucksack.**

Spelling 3 page 17

FOCUS Spelling patterns: **x** and **ex**

TEACH ▶ Ask pupils to write and show words ending with **x** (for example, **fox, box, index, relax**). Check spellings ▶ Recap the 'ks' sound usually associated with **x**. ▶ Ask pupils to use a dictionary to look for words that start with the letter **x**. Establish there are very few. ▶ Look for words that start **ex**. Establish that lots of words start **ex**, particularly **exp, ext, exc** (but rarely **exs**). ▶ Write examples on the board. ▶ Explain that the letter **x** can be confused in some words because it is influenced by other letters and pronounced 'gz' (for example, **egzaust**). Establish that thinking of these as **ex** words (rather than relying on sound) helps overcome this.

PRACTISE Spelling 3, page 17; 'Additional word list'

APPLY Spelling sentences

ASSESS Dictation: **I am excited to explore and examine the mountains.**

Spelling 3 page 18

FOCUS More 'or' spellings

TEACH ▶ *Note:* In some regions these phonemes are pronounced differently, so adapt teaching accordingly. ▶ Ask pupils to write and show familiar words: **lord, walk, saw, four, because, door, snore, thought**. ▶ Write the words on the board so pupils can check their spellings. ▶ Underline the spelling of the 'or' sound in each word. ▶ Say a special **w** word with the 'or' sound (for example, **war**). Write it on the board. ▶ Ask pupils to write **warm**. ▶ Explain that the 'or' sound has many spellings and words need to be learnt. Learning words in groups is a useful strategy (for example: **alk** words; **all** words; **war** words).

PRACTISE Spelling 3, page 18; 'Word sort 3'; 'Additional word list'

APPLY Set target (for example, spelling vowel sounds); independent writing

ASSESS Dictation: **Without warning they launched an attack from the north.**

Spelling 3 page 19

FOCUS More 'ur' spellings

TEACH ▶ Involve pupils in writing lists of rhyming words: **bird, third, heard, word; turn, churn, fern, learn; dirt, squirt, spurt, alert**. ▶ Write the easy parts (for example, **ch__n**) and discuss the spelling choice for the middle 'ur' sound. Add the correct spelling in colour (for example, **churn**). ▶ Recap and extend spelling patterns (for example: **ur, ir** and **er** are the most common; **wor** is a special pattern). ▶ Explain that the **ear** spelling of this sound is also found at the start of words (for example, **earth**).

PRACTISE Spelling 3, page 19; 'Word sort 3'

APPLY Set target; independent writing

ASSESS Dictation: **He will travel further than the end of the world in search of a worthy person.**

Spelling 3 page 20

FOCUS More 'oo' and 'yoo' spellings

TEACH ► Ask pupils to write and show: **smooth, blue, June, new.** ► Check spellings. Recap familiar spellings of the 'oo' and 'yoo' sounds. ► Add some familiar tricky words with other spellings (for example, **shoe, group**). ► Explain that some words have yet another spelling for the 'oo' sound. Say the sounds and write **fr__t** (**fruit**). ► Discuss the spelling of the vowel phoneme. If pupils suggest **oo** or **u_e**, write these in and discuss whether they look right before establishing the correct spelling and writing in the **ui** spelling in colour. ► Establish that it is important to learn words which have alternative 'oo' spellings.

PRACTISE Spelling 3, page 20; 'Word sort 3'

APPLY Independent writing; respond to marking

ASSESS Dictation: **With her super powers she will rescue the world from the cruel master.**

Spelling 3 page 21

FOCUS Topic words 3

TEACH ► Select one or two describing words from pupils' independent writing. ► Write the first word on the board (for example, **quiet**). ► Say it in a sentence. Demonstrate taking it apart by saying the sounds (or syllables, then sounds) and writing the corresponding letters. ► Identify the tricky part (**qu i et**). Discuss why it might be misspelt (confused with **quite**). ► Decide on a memory strategy, for example: stress the **et** ending to help distinguish it from **quite**. ► Ask pupils to use the chosen memory strategy to practise and remember the word. ► Cover it and ask pupils to write: All was **quiet**.

PRACTISE Spelling 3, page 21; 'Words to practise: My topic words'

APPLY Set mini-target; independent writing

ASSESS Dictation: **In the beautiful garden there was a weird ancient statue.**

Spelling 3 page 22

FOCUS Adding **y**

TEACH ► Ask pupils to write root words (for example, **rain, mist, cloud, chill, ice, sun, fog**) and change them into adjectives by adding **y**. ► Check spellings. Recap rules for adding the **y** suffix (for example: drop the **e**; double the last consonant if the root word ends short vowel and single consonant). ► Establish that these are the same rules as for adding **ing**, **ed** and other endings. ► Extend by adding **y** to words ending **le** (for example: **sparkle** – **sparkly; twinkle** – **twinkly**).

PRACTISE Spelling 3, page 22; 'Additional word list'

APPLY Set target; spelling sentences or independent writing (for example, description)

ASSESS Dictation: **The baby dragon has wrinkly skin and spotty wings and is very noisy.**

Spelling 3 page 23

FOCUS Adding **er** and **est**

TEACH ► Practise orally forming comparatives from adjectives. ► Write a root word on the board (for example, **brave**). Say: *X is **brave**; y is **braver** and z is **bravest** of all.* ► Write **braver** and **bravest** on the board. ► Repeat with other words (for example, **funny, sad**). ► Invite pupils to make up comparison sentences and to write and show the adjectives. ► Check spellings. Reinforce **er** and **est** suffixes and the changes in spelling needed to add them. ► Remind pupils the rules are the same as for adding **ed**.

PRACTISE Spelling 3, page 23; 'Additional word list'

APPLY Spelling sentences or independent writing

ASSESS Dictation: **Mina searched for the smoothest, flattest stone and Craig for the heaviest one.**

Spelling 3   page 24

FOCUS Adding **ly**

TEACH ▶ Write **proud** on the board. ▶ Say: *He walked proudly*. Write **proudly**. ▶ Discuss how the meaning changes. ▶ Repeat with **brave** (**bravely**) and **happy** (**happily**). ▶ Look at the words. Discuss changes in spelling. ▶ Establish rules: just add **ly** unless the root word ends consonant **y** – then **y** changes to **i**. Make it clear that most words ending **e** keep the **e**. ▶ Ask pupils to write and show: **sadly, lonely, merrily**. Check spellings. ▶ Introduce the **le** exception. Write **simple** and **simply**. ▶ Explain that if a word ends **le**, the **le** changes to **ly**. Reinforce that this only applies to words ending **le**; other words ending in **e** keep the **e**.

PRACTISE **Spelling 3**, page 24; 'Additional word list'

APPLY Spelling sentences or independent writing

ASSESS Dictation: **He walked <u>quietly</u> and <u>happily</u> without feeling even <u>slightly</u> <u>lonely</u>.**

Spelling 3   page 25

FOCUS Spelling words with suffixes

TEACH ▶ Recap familiar suffixes (for example, **ly, ful, y, less, er, est**). ▶ Explain that recognising the root word and the suffix can help to spell lots of longer words. ▶ Demonstrate with the word **amusement**. Say the word and ask pupils to take it apart to identify a root word and suffix. ▶ Demonstrate how to say the sounds and spelling; **amuse** and then **ment**. Read the word. ▶ Ask pupils to use the same technique to write **enjoyment**. ▶ Repeat with other words, introducing some new suffixes (for example, **enjoyable**).

PRACTISE **Spelling 3**, page 25; 'Additional word list'

APPLY Spelling sentences

ASSESS Dictation: **The <u>teacher</u> was <u>speechless</u> much to the <u>amusement</u> of the class.**

Spelling 3   page 26

FOCUS Revision 2

TEACH ▶ Use this session to reinforce rules for adding suffixes to root words. ▶ Focus on a suffix or rule pupils are having difficulty with in independent writing. ▶ Say a root word and ask pupils to write the word with the suffix. ▶ Check spellings. Discuss errors and clarify misunderstandings. ▶ Display a sentence to proof read together, checking for spelling errors associated with the suffix or rule. Ask pupils to try writing the correct spelling. ▶ Reinforce the rule that will avoid the same error in the future (for example: when to drop **e** and when to retain it; changing **y** to **i**).

PRACTISE **Spelling 3**, page 26; previous 'Additional word lists'; 'Word sort' 2 or 3

APPLY Check targets; proof reading; respond to marking

ASSESS Through independent writing

Spelling 3   page 27

FOCUS Topic words 4

TEACH ▶ Select a word relating to your current work in science (or another subject area) and write it on the board (for example, **heart, breathe**). ▶ Demonstrate taking the word apart by saying the sounds (or syllables and then sounds) and writing the corresponding letters. ▶ Identify the tricky parts (for example, **h<u>ea</u>rt, br<u>ea</u>the**). ▶ Decide on a memory strategy, for example, a visual strategy such as finding **hear** in **heart** (**hear** a **heart** beat). ▶ Ask pupils to use the memory strategy to learn the word. ▶ Cover the word and ask pupils to write: My **heart** beats.

PRACTISE **Spelling 3**, page 27; 'Words to practise: My topic words'

APPLY Set mini-target; independent writing; respond to marking

ASSESS Dictation: **Don't let a <u>young</u> pupil <u>touch</u> <u>bacteria</u>.**

Spelling 3　　　　　　　page 28

FOCUS Shortened forms 1

TEACH ▶ Use magnetic letters to form a list of pronouns: **I**, **he**, **we**, **they**. ▶ Say: *I will go.* Use the magnetic letters to form **I will**. ▶ Ask pupils to say the contracted form (**I'll go**). ▶ Demonstrate pushing the words together, taking out **wi** and putting the apostrophe in place to form **I'll**. ▶ Explain that the apostrophe replaces the missing letters; the pronoun stays the same, the verb is contracted. ▶ Repeat with **they will** (**they'll**) and **I have** (**I've**). ▶ Ask pupils to write **he'll** and **they've**.

PRACTISE **Spelling 3**, page 28; 'Word collector'

APPLY Set target; independent writing (for example, dialogue, play script, diary)

ASSESS Dictation: <u>I'm</u> a little deaf so <u>you'll</u> have to speak up or <u>I'll</u> never hear you.

Spelling 3　　　　　　　page 29

FOCUS Shortened forms 2

TEACH ▶ Ask pupils to write and show familiar examples of shortened forms (for example, **I'm**, **she'll**, **don't**). ▶ Check placement of apostrophes. Ask pupils to explain how they knew where to put the apostrophe (in place of missing letters). ▶ Say some shortened forms and ask pupils to write the full form, for example: *I'd rather not* (**I would**). ▶ Discuss which letters are replaced in the contraction. ▶ Ask pupils to write the shortened form. ▶ Repeat with other examples, such as: *he doesn't know*; *I won't do it*; *I shan't do it.* ▶ Establish that in the last two examples both words are shortened but the apostrophe goes in its familiar place (**n't**).

PRACTISE **Spelling 3**, page 29; 'Word collector'

APPLY Set target; independent writing (for example, dialogue, informal letter)

ASSESS Dictation: <u>What's</u> the matter? <u>Where's</u> Sheena? She said <u>she'd</u> call if she <u>couldn't</u> come.

Spelling 3　　　　　　　page 30

FOCUS Silent letters

TEACH ▶ Say words for pupils to write and show: **knee**, **thumb**, **write**. ▶ Check spellings. Recap familiar silent letters or unsounded consonants. ▶ Introduce words with other silent letters (for example, **listen**). ▶ Say the sounds and write the word. Identify the unsounded letter **t**. ▶ Demonstrate how saying the word as it is spelt and pronouncing the silent letter can help to spell words like this (**listen**). ▶ Cover the word so pupils can use the strategy to write it. ▶ Use the same strategy to help spell words with other unsounded consonants (for example, **g-nome**, **g-host**, **sc-issors**).

PRACTISE **Spelling 3**, page 30; 'Word collector'

APPLY Spelling sentences

ASSESS Dictation: The <u>ghastly</u> <u>ghost</u> waves his <u>sword</u> in the <u>wreckage</u> of the <u>castle</u>.

Spelling 3　　　　　　　page 31

FOCUS Soft **g** and soft **c**

TEACH ▶ Say familiar words for pupils to write and show: **giant**, **ginger**, **gentle**. ▶ Check spellings. Recap that a 'j' sound is sometimes spelt **g**. ▶ Write **ur_ent**, **en_ine**, **_ym**, **_ab**, **_umble**, **_olt**. Discuss which words have a **g** spelling and which **j**. ▶ Explain that the **g** spelling is most likely before **e**, **i** and **y**. Use this to write in the correct spelling.

Repeat the activity with some words where the 's' sound is spelt **c** (for example, **re_ipe**, **con_ert**). ▶ Establish that again the **c** spelling is usually found before **e**, **i** and **y**.

PRACTISE **Spelling 3**, page 31; 'Additional word list'

APPLY Spelling sentences

ASSESS Dictation: I <u>imagine</u> they are <u>certain</u> to <u>cancel</u> the <u>circus</u> at the <u>gym</u>.

Spelling 3   page 32

FOCUS Homophones

TEACH ▶ Write the word **grate**. Ask: *Is this the correct spelling?* ▶ Encourage discussion about the difference between **grate** and **great**. ▶ Repeat with **brake/break** and **not/knot**. ▶ Discuss what features make these words sound the same even though they have different spellings (alternative spellings of vowels sounds; silent letters). ▶ Explain that these words are called homophones (they sound the same but have different meanings and spellings) and that it is important to know the right spelling for each meaning. ▶ Say a homophone in a sentence and ask pupils to write the correct spelling, for example: *It was **great**.*

PRACTISE Spelling 3, page 32; 'Additional word list'

APPLY Spelling sentences

ASSESS Dictation: **I knew it would take the whole day to write.**

Spelling 3   page 33

FOCUS Topic words 5

TEACH ▶ Choose a term from your current English work (for example, **rhyme**) and write it on the board. ▶ Demonstrate taking the word apart by saying the sounds and writing the corresponding letters (**rh-y-me**). ▶ Identify the tricky parts and decide on a memory strategy. Rhyme is a particularly tricky word with more than one tricky part, so a mnemonic might help (for example, **r**hyme **h**elps **y**ou and **m**e). ▶ Ask pupils to use the memory strategy to practise and learn the word. ▶ Cover the word and ask pupils to write: Make it **rhyme**.

PRACTISE Spelling 3, page 33; 'Words to practise: My topic words'

APPLY Set mini-target; independent writing; respond to marking

ASSESS Dictation: **I went to fetch a dictionary from the library to help me answer the question.**

Spelling 3   page 34

FOCUS Prefixes: **re**, **de**, **pre** and **mis**

TEACH ▶ Say a word (for example, **lucky**, **agree**) and ask pupils to write and show the opposite using **un** or **dis** prefixes. ▶ Check spellings. Reinforce that prefixes change the meaning but not the spelling of a word. ▶ Use magnetic letters to make new prefixes: **re**, **pre**, **de**, **mis**. ▶ Write **fill** on the board and say: *I **fill** the glass.* ▶ Slide the **re** prefix to the start of **fill**. ▶ Discuss how the prefix changes the meaning of the word but not the spelling (**re** means again). Repeat with other words and prefixes (for example, **(pre)cook**, **(de)frost**, **(mis)count**). ▶ Establish that **pre** means before; **de** means the opposite; **mis** means wrong.

PRACTISE Spelling 3, page 34; 'Additional word list'

APPLY Set target; spelling sentences

ASSESS Dictation: **It would be a mistake to misbehave before the restart.**

Spelling 3   page 35

FOCUS More prefixes

TEACH ▶ Ask pupils, in pairs, to write and show all the prefixes they know, with example words. ▶ Check spellings. Recap that prefixes are added without any change in spelling. ▶ Ask pupils to use their knowledge of prefixes to spell a word they may not have written before (for example, **rebound**).

Introduce some other words with new prefixes such as **non**, **sub** and **anti**. Say the word and help pupils identify the prefix and the root word (for example, **nonsense**). ▶ Demonstrate writing the words on the board to show the correct spelling of the prefixes and root words.

PRACTISE Spelling 3, page 35; 'Spelling log'

APPLY Spelling sentences

ASSESS Dictation: **I am disappointed by this disgraceful mistake.**

Spelling 3   page 36

FOCUS Words ending **ture** and **sure**

TEACH ▶ Say: *picture*. Say the sounds and write the word. ▶ Establish that the second syllable sounds like 'cher' or 'chuh' but is spelt **ture**. Write over the **ture** ending in colour. ▶ Explain that there are quite a few words with this ending. ▶ Ask pupils to write another word (for example, **creature**, **mixture**).

Say the word *treasure*. Say the sounds and write the word. ▶ Establish that the second syllable sounds like 'zher' or 'zhuh' but is spelt **sure**. Write over the **sure** ending in colour. ▶ Ask pupils to write **measure**.

PRACTISE **Spelling 3**, page 36; 'Word collector'; 'Spelling log'; 'Additional word list'

APPLY Spelling sentences

ASSESS Dictation: **It was quite an <u>adventure</u> to <u>capture</u> the <u>treasure</u> from that ghastly <u>creature</u>.**

Spelling 3   page 37

FOCUS Possessive apostrophes

TEACH ▶ Practise orally using the possessive apostrophe, for example: *The ring belongs to the prince; it is the prince's ring.* ▶ Write **the prince's ring** on the board. Establish that the possessive apostrophe **'s** is added after the owner (if there is only one owner). ▶ Ask pupils to write and show: **the giant's castle**. ▶ Check correct use of apostrophe. ▶ *Note:* A common confusion is to use **'s** in plurals. If pupils do this, then write on the board: *The mans six dog's.* Ask pupils to explain what is wrong. ▶ Correct the sentence and clarify that **'s** is not used in plurals.

PRACTISE **Spelling 3**, page 37

APPLY Proof reading; respond to marking

ASSESS Dictation: **The <u>farmer's</u> <u>horses</u> were on the <u>king's</u> land.**

Spelling 3   page 38

FOCUS Revision 3

TEACH ▶ Use this session to revise any graphemes that are causing problems in independent writing (for example, a particular vowel phoneme). ▶ Show one or two sentences with typical errors. ▶ Remind pupils that good spellers proof read their writing to check for spelling errors. ▶ Read the text with pupils, looking for words that don't look right. ▶ Discuss alternative spellings and ask pupils, in pairs, to write and show what they think the correct spelling is. ▶ Check pupils' spelling. If there are errors, write the word on the board and add it to their list of tricky words to learn.

PRACTISE **Spelling 3**, page 38; 'Spelling log'

APPLY Proof reading; respond to marking

ASSESS Through independent writing

Spelling 3   page 39

FOCUS Tricky words

TEACH ▶ Focus on words pupils still misspell. ▶ Select a word to write on the board. Say the sounds; discuss the tricky bit that is misspelt and why (for example, missing a letter out (**b<u>u</u>ilding**); adding a letter in (**fami<u>ll</u>y**)). ▶ Invite pupils to explain how they would learn/remember the word. ▶ Discuss different memory strategies and let pupils decide on the one they would use for this word. ▶ Ask them to use their strategy to practise the word. Then cover the word and ask pupils to write it in a short sentence, for example: *The **building** shook.*

PRACTISE **Spelling 3**, page 39; 'Words to practise: My tricky words'

APPLY Independent writing; proof reading; respond to marking

ASSESS Dictation: **My <u>family</u> <u>used</u> to live in an old <u>building</u> <u>above</u> a <u>busy</u> shop.**

Spelling 4

Spelling 4   page 4

FOCUS Homophones 1

TEACH ▶ Say homophones for pupils to write (for example, **bare, grown, main**). ▶ Discuss why it is difficult to spell these words without a context. ▶ Give the words in sentences. Ask pupils to check and show their spellings. ▶ Check spellings; then ask pupils to write the homophone for each word (**bear, groan, mane**). ▶ Discuss the contexts in which these words might be used (for example, **mane** if writing about a lion). ▶ Orally compose example sentences. ▶ Establish that knowing the meaning of each spelling is the key strategy for remembering homophones.

PRACTISE Spelling 4, page 4; 'Additional word list'

APPLY Set target; spelling sentences; proof reading

ASSESS Dictation: **I <u>hear</u> that no high <u>heels</u> will be <u>allowed</u> on <u>board</u>.**

Spelling 4   page 5

FOCUS Homophones 2

TEACH ▶ Focus on homophones that are causing confusion (for example: **their/there; weather/whether; piece/peace**). ▶ Show flashcards for the two words. Clarify the differences in meaning, for example: **there** – about place (more general use); **their** – about people and possession (specific use). ▶ Discuss memory strategies to link meaning with spelling, for example: <u>here</u> and t<u>here</u>; w<u>he</u>ther <u>he</u> will; <u>pie</u>ce of <u>pie</u>. ▶ Say a sentence and ask pupils to point to the correct choice for that context. ▶ Discuss how their choices were made, for example: it was not about people/possession so must be **there**.

PRACTISE Spelling 4, page 5; 'Spelling log'

APPLY Personal targets; independent writing or spelling sentences

ASSESS Dictation: **I <u>knew</u> the <u>weather</u> was <u>too</u> bad <u>to</u> drive <u>through</u> the <u>night</u> in <u>their</u> old car.**

Spelling 4   page 6

FOCUS The **ch** grapheme

TEACH ▶ Ask pupils to write: **children, chew, school, ache**. ▶ Write the words on the board so they can check spellings. ▶ Recap that 'k' is sometimes spelt **ch**. ▶ Say the sounds and write on the board **chef**. Explain that a 'sh' sound is sometimes spelt **ch**. ▶ In pairs, pupils use a dictionary to locate other examples of words starting with 'k' and 'sh' sounds spelt **ch**. ▶ Write these on the board. Establish that few examples are everyday words. ▶ The 'sh' words are mainly words of French origin; 'k' words are from areas of learning, of Greek origin. This can help them remember which words use these spelling patterns.

PRACTISE Spelling 4, page 6; 'Word sort 1'

APPLY Spelling sentences

ASSESS Dictation: **The <u>chef</u> at the <u>chalet</u> in the <u>brochure</u> is quite a <u>character</u>.**

Spelling 4   page 7

FOCUS Y as a vowel

TEACH ▶ Ask pupils to write and show: **reply, worry, steady**. ▶ Check spellings. Recap the different sounds **y** can represent at the end of words ('i-e', 'ee').

Say the sounds and write on the board the words **cycle** and **myth**. Identify the sounds represented by the **y** ('i-e', 'i'). ▶ Explain that the letter **y** sometimes acts as an extra vowel within words, as well as at the end. As there are not many of these words the most useful ones can be learnt.

PRACTISE Spelling 4, page 7; 'Word sort 1'; 'Additional word list'

APPLY Spelling sentences

ASSESS Dictation: **The <u>mystery</u> of the <u>python</u> in the <u>pyramid</u>. Is it just a <u>myth</u>?**

Spelling 4 page 8

FOCUS The apostrophe test

TEACH ▶ Some contractions cause particular confusion, for example: **its**, **it's**; **were**, **we're**; **their**, **they're**. Focus on one pupils are having difficulty with. ▶ Hold up flashcards with the two forms (for example, **it's**, **its**). Clarify the differences: **it's** – short for 'it is' (or 'it has'); **its** – means belonging to it (like 'his'). ▶ Explain that there should only be an apostrophe if **its** can be replaced with 'it is' or 'it has'. ▶ Say a sentence and ask pupils to use this test to point to the right spelling, for example: *It's late. The book had lost its cover.*

PRACTISE **Spelling 4**, page 8; 'Mini spelling log'

APPLY Spelling sentences or respond to marking

ASSESS Dictation: <u>We're</u> certain <u>their</u> car was left in <u>its</u> parking space.

Spelling 4 page 9

FOCUS Tricky words

TEACH ▶ Write on the board a word that frequently trips up pupils when writing (for example, **favourite**). ▶ Follow the sequence of taking it apart (breaking it into syllables and/or phonemes), identifying the difficult part and choosing a way to remember it. ▶ Encourage pupils to explain why they misspell the word (for example, **favorite**). ▶ Discuss memory strategies to overcome the problem, for example: visual (look for **our**); sound (say: *fav-our-ite*); remember (<u>our</u> fav<u>our</u>ite).

PRACTISE **Spelling 4**, page 9; 'Words to practise: My tricky words'

APPLY Set mini-target; independent writing

ASSESS Dictation: **Walk <u>forwards</u> <u>forty</u> paces. Make <u>sure</u> you keep to the <u>actual</u> path.**

Spelling 4 page 10

FOCUS Tricky plurals 1

TEACH ▶ Say a list of plurals for pupils to write and show (for example, **ferns**, **bushes**, **roses**, **grasses**, **daisies**). ▶ Check spellings. Recap rules for spelling plurals (for example: add **s**; add **es**; change **y** to **i** and add **es**). ▶ Write **leaf**. ▶ Discuss what happens to words ending **f** or **fe**. Write **leaves**. ▶ Establish that in most cases **f/fe** is dropped and **ves** is added. (But words ending **ff**, just add **s**, for example, **cuffs**.) ▶ Explain that there are exceptions (for example, **roofs**, **chiefs**). Emphasise a 'fs' sound at the end of these words to distinguish them.

PRACTISE **Spelling 4**, page 10; 'Additional word list'

APPLY Set target; spelling sentences

ASSESS Dictation: **The <u>calves</u> saw the <u>wolves</u> and ran for their <u>lives</u>.**

Spelling 4 page 11

FOCUS Tricky plurals 2

TEACH ▶ Write a list of animals. Write the singular and ask pupils to write and show the plural: **camel/s**, **fox/es**, **wolf/wolves**, **panda/s**, **rhino/s**. ▶ Check spellings. Recap rules for forming plurals. ▶ Discuss words ending with **o**. Explain that they often just add **s** (for example, **rhinos**) but that some older words add **es** (for example, **tomatoes**, **potatoes**). ▶ Continue the list by writing **mouse**, **goose** and **deer**. ▶ Discuss the plurals of these words (**mice**, **geese**, **deer**). Explain that some words do not follow the normal **s/es** pattern – these are called 'irregular plurals'.

PRACTISE **Spelling 4**, page 11; 'Additional word list'

APPLY Spelling sentences

ASSESS Dictation: **The <u>women</u> laughed at the two <u>gentlemen</u> in their fine <u>clothes</u>.**

Spelling 4   page 12

FOCUS Spelling patterns **gu** and **gue**

TEACH ▶ Say the sounds and write the words **guess** (**gu/e/ss**) and **guide** (**gu/i/d/e**). ▶ In colour, write over the **gu** spelling of 'g'. Explain that the unsounded **u** helps keep the 'g' as a hard sound (rather than a soft 'j' sound). ▶ Ask pupils to write and show **guest**.

Now say the sounds and write the word **vague** (**v-a-gu-e**). ▶ In colour, write over the **gue** spelling of 'g'. Explain that this spelling of 'g' is found at the end of some words. It is necessary to learn which words have this spelling. ▶ Ask pupils to write other words with this spelling (for example, **league**).

PRACTISE **Spelling 4**, page 12; 'Additional word list'

APPLY Spelling sentences

ASSESS Dictation: **I was <u>intrigued</u> to see the <u>guests</u> had an armed <u>guard</u>.**

Spelling 4   page 13

FOCUS Spelling patterns **qu** and **que**

TEACH ▶ Ask pupils to write and show: **question**, **squelch**, **squash**. ▶ Check spellings. Recap 'qu' and 'squ' sounds and spellings and the **w** special rules that apply after 'kw' sounds. ▶ Ask pupils to write **squad** and **equal**.

Now say the sounds and write **mosque** on the board. Establish that the 'k' sound is spelt **que**. Write over **que** in colour. ▶ Explain that words with this spelling are often of French origin and they need to be learnt. ▶ Ask pupils to write another word with this pattern (for example, **antique**).

PRACTISE **Spelling 4**, page 13; 'Additional word list'

APPLY Spelling sentences

ASSESS Dictation: **The <u>grotesque</u> monsters started to <u>quarrel</u> over the <u>quantity</u> of <u>liquid</u>.**

Spelling 4   page 14

FOCUS Revision 1

TEACH ▶ Use this session to revise spelling patterns which pupils are having difficulty with in their independent writing. ▶ This might be alternative ways of representing a particular vowel or consonant or an ending that is not spelt as it sounds (for example, **le**, **tion**, **ture**, **sure**). ▶ Say the sounds and write an example on the board as a model. ▶ Say other words with the same pattern and help pupils write these.

PRACTISE **Spelling 4**, page 14; 'Words to practise: Spelling practice ladders'

APPLY Proof reading; respond to marking

ASSESS Through independent writing

Spelling 4   page 15

FOCUS Topic words 1

TEACH ▶ Choose a term from your current maths work and write it on the board (for example, **horizontal**). ▶ Demonstrate saying the syllables (**ho/ri/zon/tal**) and then saying the sounds in each syllable as you write the corresponding letters. ▶ Look at the word broken down and identify any parts that are still tricky (for example, **al** ending). ▶ Decide on a way to remember it, for example: say **ho/ri/zon/<u>tal</u>** to make the **al** spelling clear. ▶ Cover the word and ask pupils to use this strategy to write the word.

PRACTISE **Spelling 4**, page 15; 'Words to practise: My topic words'

APPLY Set mini-target; independent writing

ASSESS Dictation: **I <u>estimate</u> it will <u>probably</u> take a <u>minute</u> for the lift to <u>descend</u>.**

Spelling 4   page 16

FOCUS Letter strings: **ear**

TEACH ▶ Explain that a letter string is a sequence of letters often seen in words. ▶ On the board, write **ear**. ▶ Invite examples of words with this letter string. ▶ List words according to pronunciation to establish that the **ear** letter strings represent a variety of sounds (for example: 'ear' – **hear**, **appear**; 'air' – **bear**, **pear**; 'ur' – **learn**, **earth**). ▶ Explain that learning visual patterns like this helps when checking if a word looks right (for example, recognising likely (and unlikely) sequences of letters). ▶ Another useful visual technique is to look for a word within a word (for example, **earth**). ▶ Ask pupils to write **yearn**.

PRACTISE Spelling 4, page 16; 'Additional word list'

APPLY Spelling sentences

ASSESS Dictation: **It** <u>appears</u> **to be such a** <u>dreary</u> **day, I will end this** <u>weary</u> <u>search</u> <u>early</u>**.**

Spelling 4   page 17

FOCUS Letter strings: **gh**

TEACH ▶ Ask pupils to write and show: **light**, **night**, **high**. ▶ Check spellings. Recap **igh** (long 'i'). ▶ Ask for words where **igh** does not represent long 'i' (for example, **eight**, **weigh**). Write the words on the board. ▶ Explain that **e** before **igh** usually changes the sound. ▶ Ask pupils to practise writing **eigh** to fix the letter string in the memory. ▶ Repeat with **aught** or **ought** letter strings. Discuss the pronunciation when **gh** is combined with these other letters. ▶ Let pupils practise writing **aught** or **ought**. ▶ Establish that it can be helpful to look at these as visual (rather than sound) patterns and train the hand to write and the brain to remember them, particularly as there are many exceptions (for example, **height**).

PRACTISE Spelling 4, page 17; 'Word collector'

APPLY Spelling sentences

ASSESS Dictation: **My** <u>naughty</u> <u>daughter</u> <u>bought</u> **a new car, much to her** <u>delight</u>**.**

Spelling 4   page 18

FOCUS Prefixes **al**, **a**, **ad** and **be**

TEACH ▶ Ask pupils to write words with familiar prefixes (for example, **before**, **mishear**, **nonsense**). ▶ Check spellings. Recap that adding prefixes needs no change to the root word. ▶ Write on the board **always** and **allways**. ▶ Discuss the correct spelling and then rub out **allways**. ▶ Explain that **all** as a prefix is spelt **al** (like **ful** as a suffix). ▶ Write over **al** in colour to show clearly the prefix and the root word (<u>al</u>ways). ▶ Repeat with **addverb/adverb** and **affloat/afloat**. ▶ Establish that the prefixes are **ad** and **a**. Ask pupils to spell other words with these prefixes (for example, **ajar**, **also**, **advent**).

PRACTISE Spelling 4, page 18; 'Word collector'

APPLY Independent writing

ASSESS Dictation: <u>Although</u> **he was** <u>already</u> **late he stopped** <u>awhile</u> <u>beneath</u> **a shady tree.**

Spelling 4   page 19

FOCUS Detecting prefixes

TEACH ▶ Ask pupils, in pairs, to write and show prefixes they know, with example words. ▶ Check spellings. ▶ Say some words with unfamiliar prefixes (for example, **imperfect**, **incorrect**). ▶ Ask pupils to identify the root word and the prefix. ▶ Discuss how the prefix changes the meaning of the root word. ▶ Write the words on the board, writing the prefix and then root word. Recap that there is no change of spelling when a prefix is added. ▶ Write the prefixes in colour so pupils learn to recognise them in other words. ▶ Discuss how recognising prefixes helps to spell words.

PRACTISE Spelling 4, page 19; 'Additional word list'

APPLY Spelling sentences

ASSESS Dictation: **It may be** <u>imperfect</u>**, but we still** <u>approve</u> **the plan for the** <u>surrounding</u> **parkland.**

Spelling 4 — page 20

FOCUS Adding **ly**

TEACH ► Ask pupils to write **bravely**, **safely**, **gently** and **really**. ► Write each word on the board so pupils can check their spellings. ► Use this opportunity to clarify common confusions with adding **ly** (for example, whether to keep or drop the **e**). ► Recap the main rule (just add **ly** even if the word ends **e**) and the exception for words ending **le** (**le** is changed to **ly**). ► Explain that this makes the resulting word easier to say. ► Clarify also that the just add **ly** rule still applies if the root word ends with **l**, but this results in double **l** (for example, **really**).

PRACTISE Spelling 4, page 20; 'Additional word list'

APPLY Proof reading; respond to marking; check targets

ASSESS Dictation: **It was <u>totally</u>, <u>completely</u> and quite <u>simply</u> brilliant.**

Spelling 4 — page 21

FOCUS Topic words 2

TEACH ► Select a word relating to current science work (or another subject area), for example, **material**. Write it on the board. ► Demonstrate taking it apart by saying the syllables and then the sounds for each syllable and writing the corresponding letters (for example, **ma/te/ri/al**). ► Identify the tricky parts (for example, **ri/al**). ► Decide on a memory strategy, for example: say the syllables and stress the **ri-<u>al</u>** ending. ► Ask pupils to use the memory strategy to learn the word. ► Cover the word and ask pupils to write a short phrase (for example, **fireproof material**).

PRACTISE Spelling 4, page 21; 'Words to practise: My topic words'

APPLY Set mini-target; independent writing in science

ASSESS Dictation: **I drew a <u>diagram</u> of an <u>electric</u> <u>circuit</u> with a <u>battery</u>, a buzzer and a switch.**

Spelling 4 — page 22

FOCUS Adding **ed** and **ing**

TEACH ► Practise changing verb tense using **ing** and **ed**. ► Write a two-syllable verb on the board (for example, **reply**). ► Say: *I am replying. I replied.* Ask pupils to write and show the verbs. ► Repeat with other words (for example, **relax**, **approve**, **admit**). ► Check spellings, revising rules for adding **ing** and **ed** (dropping **e**; consonant doubling; **y** to **i**). ► On the board, write **listen** then **listening** and **listened**. Underline the **<u>en</u>** syllable. ► Explain that because this syllable is difficult to hear (unstressed) the last consonant (**n**) is not doubled. ► Ask pupils to follow the pattern to write **glistened** and **glistening**.

PRACTISE Spelling 4, page 22; 'Additional word list'

APPLY Set targets; independent writing; proof reading

ASSESS Dictation: **They <u>hurried</u> home, <u>forgetting</u> what had <u>happened</u> in that <u>terrifying</u> moment.**

Spelling 4 — page 23

FOCUS Adjective suffixes

TEACH ► Make a list of familiar adjective suffixes (for example, **ful**, **less**, **y**, **able**). ► Ask pupils to write and show: **truthful**, **hopeless**, **muddy**. ► Check spelling of suffixes, root words and changes needed. ► Add more suffixes to the list: **al**, **ic**, **ive**. ► Write **music** and add **al** in colour. Say *music/al*, first stressing the **al** suffix and then as it would be pronounced normally. Repeat with other words (for example, **rhythm/ic**, **expens(e)/ive**). ► Ask pupils to write **magical**. ► Discuss how knowing the suffix **al** helped to spell the word.

PRACTISE Spelling 4, page 23; 'Additional word list'

APPLY Spelling sentences or independent writing

ASSESS Dictation: **This <u>historic</u> castle, with so many <u>attractive</u> features, is a <u>national</u> treasure.**

Spelling 4 page 24

FOCUS Verb suffixes

TEACH ► Use magnetic letters to form **en**, **ify**, **ate** and **ise**. Explain that these suffixes change words into verbs. ► Write **tight**, then slide **en** into place at the end. Say *tight/en* (first stress the suffix, then say the word normally). ► Show that it is a verb. Say: *I can't **tight** a screw top but I can **tighten** it.* ► Repeat with **decor/ate**, **simpl(e)/ify** and **energ(y)/ise**, demonstrating how to drop the **e** and **y** to add the suffix. ► Rub off each word in turn and ask pupils to write it, thinking about the root word and suffix. ► Discuss how knowing about these suffixes helped them to spell the words.

PRACTISE Spelling 4, page 24; 'Spelling log'

APPLY Spelling sentences

ASSESS Dictation: **We must strengthen the team, tighten the defence and try to equalise.**

Spelling 4 page 25

FOCUS Forming nouns

TEACH ► Display a list of noun suffixes: **ness**, **ment**, **ship**, **dom**, **hood**, **age**, **ist**, **ity**. ► Read through the list. Identify noun suffixes and vowel suffixes. ► Discuss how knowing about suffixes helps to spell longer words (for example: recognising suffixes on the end of words and knowing how they are spelt; knowing rules for adding suffixes). ► Ask pupils to use the list to write and show words you say (for example, **kindness**, **shortage**, **freedom**, **nastiness**, **purity**). ► Check spellings and clarify changes in spelling when adding suffixes (for example, drop the **y** to add a suffix).

PRACTISE Spelling 4, page 25; 'Additional word list'

APPLY Spelling sentences

ASSESS Dictation: **It was his stupidity, meanness and laziness that lost him his kingdom.**

Spelling 4 page 26

FOCUS Revision 2

TEACH ► Recap the importance of knowing how to spell suffixes and how to add them to root words. ► Say words for pupils to write and show. Choose words to focus on suffixes and rules that pupils are having difficulty with. ► Check spellings and discuss errors. ► Identify why errors are made (for example: spelling the root word incorrectly; spelling the suffix incorrectly; an error in adding the suffix to the root word) and what rule or guideline will help correct it.

PRACTISE Spelling 4, page 26; 'Spelling log'

APPLY Proof reading; respond to marking; check targets

ASSESS Through independent writing

Spelling 4 page 27

FOCUS Topic words 3

TEACH ► Choose words relating to current work in another subject area, such as geography. Write one on the board. ► Ask pupils how they would take the word apart in order to learn to spell it (for example: say the sounds; say the syllables; identify the root word and prefix or suffix). ► Take the word apart and identify tricky parts (for example, where a sound is not clear or is spelt in an unexpected way). ► Discuss a suitable memory strategy (for example, say **ve-hi-cle**). ► Ask pupils to use the strategies discussed to practise and then write the word.

PRACTISE Spelling 4, page 27; 'Words to practise: My topic words'

APPLY Set mini-target; independent writing in subject area

ASSESS Dictation: **In an urban environment there are many more factories, vehicles and buildings than in the country.**

Spelling 4 — page 28

FOCUS Adding **ation**

TEACH ► Ask pupils to write and show: **fiction**, **action**, **station**, **mention**. ► Recap that 'shun' endings are spelt **tion**. ► On the board write the verb **inform**, then add **ation**. ► Use both words in context to show a verb has been changed into a noun (for example: I will **inform** you when the **information** arrives). ► Explain that **ation** is a suffix that changes verbs into nouns. ► Ask pupils to write **tempt** and add **ation**. Invite them to use the word in sentences. ► Repeat with the words **invite** and **vary** to show that the 'drop the **e**' and '**y** to **i**' rules apply with this suffix.

PRACTISE **Spelling 4**, page 28; 'Spelling log'

APPLY Spelling sentences

ASSESS Dictation: **I have great <u>admiration</u> for his <u>determination</u> to reach the final <u>destination</u>.**

Spelling 4 — page 29

FOCUS Words ending 'shun'

TEACH ► Say the syllables and write **add/i/tion** and **sub/trac/tion**. Underline the **tion** suffix. ► Repeat with **di/vi/sion**. Underline the **sion** spelling. ► Explain that while **tion** is the more common spelling, the **sion** spelling occurs in special cases. ► Discuss and write the root verb for **division** (**divide**). ► Explain that the clue comes in the last letter or letters of the root word. If it ends **d/de** or **s/se** then the spelling is **sion** (for example, **revise** – **revision**). Repeat with **express/ion** to show that if the verb ends **ss** the 'shun' spelling is **ssion**.

PRACTISE **Spelling 4**, page 29; 'Additional word list'

APPLY Spelling sentences

ASSESS Dictation: **On <u>reflection</u>, the <u>decision</u> caused a mixed <u>reaction</u> and some <u>confusion</u>.**

Spelling 4 — page 30

FOCUS Words ending **ous** and **ious**

TEACH ► Say *enormous*. Say the syllables and write **e/nor/m___**. ► Discuss the final syllable. Explain that the final 'us' sound is spelt **ous**; it is a suffix found at the end of many adjectives. ► Write it in, in colour. ► Write **fame** and add **ous** to demonstrate dropping the **e** to add **ous** (**famous**). ► Write **glory** and add **ous** (**glorious**) to show that **y** changes to **i**. ► Say the word slowly to show that there is an **i** sound before the **ous**. Explain that this helps to distinguish **ious** from **ous** words even if there is no root word. ► Ask pupils to write and show **serious**.

PRACTISE **Spelling 4**, page 30; 'Spelling log'

APPLY Spelling sentences

ASSESS Dictation: **It was <u>obvious</u> he was <u>jealous</u> of my <u>fabulous</u> costume.**

Spelling 4 — page 31

FOCUS Words ending **able** and **ible**

TEACH ► Write the words **breakable** and **terrible**. ► Underline the **ible** and **able** endings. Establish that these endings sound the same in normal speech. ► Explain patterns that help distinguish the two. For example, **able** is the more common, particularly if it follows a complete word. Demonstrate this by covering **able** to leave the word **break**. ► Explain that **ible** is more common if there is no complete root word. Cover **ible** to leave **terr**. ► Write **sensible**. Explain that **ible** often follows the letter **s** even if there is a recognisable root word. ► Ask pupils to write and show **possible** and **washable**.

PRACTISE **Spelling 4**, page 31; 'Additional word list'

APPLY Spelling sentences or independent writing

ASSESS Dictation: **The room was <u>terrible</u>, the food was barely <u>edible</u> and the weather was <u>miserable</u>.**

Spelling 4 — page 32

FOCUS The possessive apostrophe: plurals

TEACH ▶ Write a list of plurals (for example, **wolves, pupils, people**). ▶ Use the words to show examples of the possessive apostrophe (for example: **the wolves' den; pupils' toys**). ▶ Establish that if the owner is a plural that ends in s, the apostrophe is added after the s; if the owner is an irregular plural with no s, then 's is added to the end. ▶ Clarify that the 's relates to possession, not to there being more than one — plurals do not need apostrophes. ▶ Recap the two uses of the apostrophe: missing letters in shortened forms and possession. ▶ Devise tests to use when writing, for example: *Ask yourself, is it a shortened form? Does it show possession?*

PRACTISE **Spelling 4**, page 32; 'Word sort 1'

APPLY Proof reading; respond to marking

ASSESS Dictation: **All the <u>children's</u> lunchboxes were left in their <u>mothers'</u> cars.**

Spelling 4 — page 33

FOCUS Topic words 4

TEACH ▶ Select a word relating to current work in English. Write it on the board. ▶ Ask pupils how they would take the word apart to learn to spell it (for example: say the syllables or sounds; identify the root word and prefix or suffix). ▶ Follow pupils' suggestions to write the word on the board. Identify any tricky parts (for example, an unclear sound or unexpected spelling). ▶ Discuss a suitable memory strategy for the tricky part. ▶ Ask pupils to use the strategies discussed to practise spelling the word.

PRACTISE **Spelling 4**, page 33; 'Words to practise: My topic words'

APPLY Set mini-targets; writing in English

ASSESS Dictation: **The comma, <u>apostrophe</u> and <u>exclamation</u> mark are all types of <u>punctuation</u>.**

Spelling 4 — page 34

FOCUS Say the syllables

TEACH ▶ Ask pupils to write and show **Wednesday** and **important**. ▶ Check spellings, particularly the unstressed syllables. ▶ Ask pupils to demonstrate how they said the words to help spell them (for example, **Wed/<u>nes</u>/day**). ▶ Explain that saying the syllables and stressing the hidden part is a useful strategy for words that have letters or syllables that are difficult to hear when pronounced normally. ▶ Practise using this strategy with other words (for example, **listening, benefit**).

PRACTISE **Spelling 4**, page 34; 'Spelling log'

APPLY Set target; independent writing

ASSESS Dictation: **This <u>property</u> is of <u>generous</u> size with many <u>interesting</u> features.**

Spelling 4 — page 35

FOCUS Detecting roots and affixes

TEACH ▶ Ask pupils to write and show five prefixes and five suffixes. ▶ Introduce the term 'affix'. ▶ Discuss how knowing about affixes helps to spell words (for example: breaking down or building up a word; thinking of words in terms of root words and affixes). ▶ Demonstrate writing a word with both a prefix and a suffix (for example, **unforgivable, unhappily**). ▶ Explain the changes in spelling as suffixes are added. ▶ Invite pupils to use the same strategy to write another word (for example, **disappointed**).

PRACTISE **Spelling 4**, page 35; 'Additional word list'

APPLY Set target; independent writing

ASSESS Dictation: **The <u>replacement</u> is <u>unbreakable</u> and <u>inexpensive</u>.**

Spelling 4   page 36

FOCUS Word families

TEACH ▶ Explain that many words in the English language are derived from other words. ▶ Write the word **children**. Explain that **child** is the root word (the basic word with no affixes). ▶ Discuss other words with the same root and write them on the board (for example, **childlike**). ▶ Explain that this is a word family – a group of words with a common root word, linked by meaning. ▶ Write the word **once**. Identify the root **one**. ▶ Discuss how thinking about root words and word families gives a clue to spelling.

PRACTISE **Spelling 4**, page 36; 'Word collector'

APPLY Spelling sentences

ASSESS Dictation: **After <u>breakfast</u>, I will <u>request</u> an <u>example</u> of the <u>design</u> for the <u>medical</u> centre.**

Spelling 4   page 37

FOCUS Greek and Latin prefixes

TEACH ▶ Explain that the English language has many words that come from Latin and Greek roots. ▶ Write **tele**. Ask for three words that start with this root. ▶ Write the words on the board, clarifying how they are built from roots (for example, **tele vision**, **tele scope**, **tele phone**). ▶ Help pupils work out the meaning of **tele** (far off). Discuss how this relates to the meaning of the words on the board. ▶ Cover the words and ask pupils to write them. ▶ Discuss how thinking about the root helped them to spell the word. ▶ Could they spell another **tele** word (for example, **teleport**)?

PRACTISE **Spelling 4**, page 37; 'Additional word list'

APPLY Spelling sentences

ASSESS Dictation: **The spy hid a <u>miniature</u> <u>microphone</u> in the <u>television</u> to <u>transmit</u> messages.**

Spelling 4   page 38

FOCUS Revision 3

TEACH ▶ Ask pupils to explain what they have learnt about spelling longer words. ▶ Encourage them to describe how they might use word structure (root words and affixes) and links to other related words, as well as the usual sound strategies such as breaking words into syllables. ▶ On the board, write words spelt incorrectly and discuss which strategy would be most helpful to correct each one (for example, **mikrowave**, **dissappoint**, **benafit**).

PRACTISE **Spelling 4**, page 38; 'Words to practise: Spelling practice ladders'

APPLY Respond to marking; proof reading; check targets

ASSESS Through independent writing

Spelling 4   page 39

FOCUS Topic words 5

TEACH ▶ Display a list of school subjects. Ask pupils to identify one they think is tricky. ▶ Follow the sequence of taking the word apart (breaking it into syllables or sounds or word parts). ▶ Identify the potentially difficult part, for example: an unusual spelling pattern (**geo**); a hidden syllable or tricky ending (**lit/<u>er</u>/a/cy**); a double letter (**a<u>ss</u>embly**). ▶ Discuss strategies to help remember the correct spelling, for example: say the syllables in **lit/er/a/cy**; say it as it's spelt (**ge-o-graphy**).

PRACTISE **Spelling 4**, page 39; 'Words to practise: My topic words'

APPLY Set mini-target; independent writing

ASSESS Dictation: **After <u>registration</u> the <u>junior</u> pupils used to go into <u>assembly</u>.**

Spelling 5

Spelling 5   page 4

FOCUS Unstressed vowels 1

TEACH ▶ Ask pupils to write and show: **interesting, benefit, different, separate, chocolate**. Check spellings. Recap spelling words with vowels that are unstressed (not clear) when words are pronounced normally. ▶ Demonstrate how saying the syllables and using exaggerated pronunciation helps make the unstressed vowels clear (for example, **ben/e/fit**). ▶ On the board, write other words with unstressed vowels and endings (for example, **definite, general, manage, bargain**). ▶ Identify the unstressed part together and ask pupils to use the strategies to say and write the words.

PRACTISE Spelling 5, page 4; 'Spelling log'

APPLY Set target; independent writing

ASSESS Dictation: **We are considering several similar ideas that we hope will become popular.**

Spelling 5   page 5

FOCUS Unstressed vowels 2

TEACH ▶ Write on the board: **frightening, cookery, freedom**. Say the words as they are normally spoken. ▶ Identify the unstressed vowels. ▶ Write each word as a sum showing the root word and suffix or suffixes (**cook + er + y; fright + en + ing; free + dom**). ▶ Discuss how this strategy helps reveal the unstressed vowels in endings or in the middle of words where two suffixes are added. ▶ Write another word on the board (for example, **considerable**). Ask pupils to use the word structure strategy to spell it correctly.

PRACTISE Spelling 5, page 5; 'Spelling log'

APPLY Independent writing; respond to marking

ASSESS Dictation: **Tomorrow they will be offering a considerable sum of money for the original works of art.**

Spelling 5   page 6

FOCUS Words ending 'er'

TEACH ▶ Ask pupils to write and show: **father, actor, centre, collar**. ▶ Check spellings. Establish that the endings all sound like 'er' but some are spelt differently (**or, re, ar**). ▶ On the board, write the start of other nouns (for example, **bak__, visit__, gramm__**). Discuss the correct endings. ▶ Group the words according to the spelling. Look for helpful patterns (for example: **er** is most common for traditional jobs or activities; **or** for newer jobs and activities; **re** in some maths terms). ▶ Establish that some words must be learnt and that stressing the endings is helpful (**ac-tor**).

PRACTISE Spelling 5, page 6; 'Additional word list'

APPLY Spelling sentences

ASSESS Dictation: **The inventor showed the professor the solar calendar on her computer monitor.**

Spelling 5   page 7

FOCUS Words ending **ary, ory** and **ery**

TEACH ▶ Ask pupils to write and show: **January, factory, cookery**. ▶ Check spellings, focusing on endings. Establish that in normal speech it is difficult to distinguish between **ary, ory** and **ery** (the vowel is unstressed). ▶ Discuss strategies to help remember the correct spellings, for example: say the syllables and use exaggerated pronunciation of the ending (**Jan-u-a-ry; fact-or-y**); use word structure (for example, **cook/er/y**). ▶ On the board, write three more words (for example, **burglary, memory, gallery**). Discuss how the above strategies would help to spell them.

PRACTISE Spelling 5, page 7; 'Additional word list'

APPLY Independent writing or spelling sentences

ASSESS Dictation: **It was an interesting discovery in the directory that finally helped solve the mystery in the gallery.**

Spelling 5   page 8

FOCUS Words ending 'shun'

TEACH ► Randomly display the words **reduce**, **reduction**; **inflate**, **inflation**; **explode**, **explosion**; **revise**, **revision**; **magic**, **magician**; **discuss**, **discussion**; **admit**, **admission**. ► Ask pupils to pair up the verbs and nouns. ► Explain that the clue to the 'shun' spellings is in the last letter of the root word. Discuss patterns, for example: **tion** is used if root word ends **t**, **te**, **ate**; **sion** if root word ends **d/de** or **s/se**; **ssion** if root word ends **ss** or **it**; **cian** if root word ends with **c** (often jobs). ► Note that sometimes a letter is added before the **tion** (for example, ad<u>d</u>i<u>t</u>ion, revo<u>l</u>u<u>t</u>ion), but these spellings are clearly pronounced.

PRACTISE Spelling 5, page 8; 'Additional word list'

APPLY Spelling sentences or independent writing

ASSESS Dictation: **They made a <u>decision</u> to ask <u>permission</u> to change <u>direction</u> and visit the <u>optician</u>.**

Spelling 5   page 9

FOCUS Tricky words

TEACH ► Explain that it is not just long complicated words that cause problems; some short words can be just as troublesome. ► On the board, write a short tricky word that pupils frequently get wrong (for example, **ninth**). Discuss why the word causes problems and might be misspelt (for example, spelling it **nineth**). ► Explain that words like these need to be learnt. Discuss possible strategies for pupils to try, for example: say **nin-th** rather than **nine-th**; look at and write it a number of times, so **ninth** looks right and **nineth** looks wrong.

PRACTISE Spelling 5, page 9; 'Words to practise: My tricky words'

APPLY Set mini-target; independent writing

ASSESS Dictation: **I was <u>eighth</u> in the <u>queue</u> of people that stretched into the <u>forest</u>.**

Spelling 5   page 10

FOCUS Letter string **au**

TEACH ► Ask pupils to write and show: **haunt**, **laugh**, **aunt**, **cause**. ► Check spellings. Establish that all the words contain the **au** letter string. ► Discuss which of the words have an 'aw' sound (**haunt**, **cause**) and which have a different sound (**aunt**, **laugh**). ► Recap that letter strings like **au** can represent different sounds, so visual strategies rather than sound spelling are helpful when spelling these words. Discuss helpful visual strategies, such as linking **aunt** to **haunt** even though they don't sound the same.

PRACTISE Spelling 5, page 10; 'Word sort 1'

APPLY Set target; spelling sentences

ASSESS Dictation: **The <u>beautiful</u> <u>daughter</u> <u>laughed</u> and gave a <u>haughty</u> toss of her hair when she saw the pile of <u>laundry</u>.**

Spelling 5   page 11

FOCUS Letter string **our**

TEACH ► Ask pupils to write and show: **our**, **four**, **colour**. Establish that although they sound different all these words contain the **our** letter string. ► Invite pupils to suggest other words with this letter string. List them on the board according to pronunciation, for example: **our**, **flour**; **your**, **four**; **colour**, **flavour**. ► Discuss patterns in pronunciation and position in the word (for example, the sound at the end of two-syllable words such as **colour** and **flavour**). ► Establish strategies for remembering how to spell these words, for example: looking for the little word **our**; saying **our** as you write it.

PRACTISE Spelling 5, page 11; 'Additional word list'

APPLY Spelling sentences

ASSESS Dictation: **The ship changed <u>course</u> after leaving the <u>harbour</u> on a <u>detour</u> to its <u>favourite</u> <u>journey</u>.**

Spelling 5   page 12

FOCUS Letter string **ough**

TEACH ▶ Ask pupils to write: **thought, cough, although**. ▶ Write the words on the board so pupils can check them. Establish that the words all contain the letter string **ough** and that in each word it represents a different sound. ▶ Discuss other words containing **ough**. Write them on the board. ▶ Establish that the only consistent sound pattern is **ought** (for 'or-t' sound). ▶ With the other **ough** words, visual and memory strategies are more helpful, because there are only a few words with each pronunciation. ▶ On the board, write **th_r_ _ _ _**. Discuss what **ough** word it could be.

PRACTISE Spelling 5, page 12; 'Spelling log'

APPLY Spelling sentences or independent writing

ASSESS Dictation: **The snowplough did a thorough job around the borough all through winter.**

Spelling 5   page 13

FOCUS Words with **ie** and **ei**

TEACH ▶ Ask pupils to write and show: **chief, grief, believe**. ▶ Check spellings. Recap the **ie** spelling of long 'e' sound. ▶ Say the sounds and write **receive** (**re-c-ei-ve**). Explain that if the long 'e' sound follows **c** it is spelt **ei** rather than **ie**. ▶ Ask pupils to write **ceiling**. ▶ Warn pupils about exceptions (for example, **weird**) which must be learnt as tricky words (for example, using a memory trick like **we** are **wei**rd).

Discuss words where **ie** or **ei** represents a different sound (for example, **friend, quiet, eight, neigh**). ▶ Write these on the board in two columns (**ei** and **ie**). Discuss patterns, for example: **ei** at the start of words; **ei** and **eigh** for an 'ay' sound.

PRACTISE Spelling 5, page 13; 'Additional word list'

APPLY Independent writing; respond to marking

ASSESS Dictation: **It will be a relief to finally achieve my target and receive the reward.**

Spelling 5   page 14

FOCUS Revision 1

TEACH ▶ Focus on an area causing problems in independent writing (for example, unstressed vowels or a particular letter string). ▶ Write a few sentences on the board to demonstrate proof reading for errors relating to the focus. ▶ Involve pupils in identifying errors (for example, explaining why a word looks wrong and suggesting alternative spellings). Demonstrate writing alternative spellings to see which looks right, and using other sources to find the correct spelling. ▶ Reinforce strategies taught earlier to help avoid similar errors.

PRACTISE Spelling 5, page 14; 'Words to practise: Spelling practice ladders'

APPLY Proof reading; respond to marking; check targets

ASSESS Through independent writing

Spelling 5   page 15

FOCUS Topic words 1

TEACH ▶ Select terms relating to your current work in geography or another subject area. Write one or two words on the board (for example, **facility, region**). ▶ Involve pupils in taking the word apart to identify the potential tricky parts (for example, **fa/cil/i/ty, re/gion**). ▶ Ask pupils to suggest memory strategies to help remember the tricky parts (for example: stressing or overemphasising in pronunciation (**it/y**); saying it as it's spelt (**re/gi-on**); linking it to another word; looking for a word within a word). Help pupils select and use a strategy to remember and write the word.

PRACTISE Spelling 5, page 15; 'Words to practise: My topic words'

APPLY Set mini-target; independent writing in subject area

ASSESS Dictation: **What leisure facilities are there for the local inhabitants in this region?**

Spelling 5   page 16

(FOCUS) Words with soft **c**

(TEACH) ▶ Ask pupils to write: **recite**, **concentrate**, **cycle**, **success**. ▶ Write the words on the board so pupils can check spellings. ▶ Establish that a 's' sound is spelt **c** in these words. ▶ Discuss guidelines for this spelling pattern. Establish that soft **c** spelling is usually found before the letters **i**, **e** and **y**. Write over **ci**, **cy** and **ce** in colour. ▶ On the board, write words with missing 's' sounds, for example: **ex_eed** (exceed); **fa_ _inate** (fascinate); **_u_pect** (suspect). ▶ Discuss the spelling in each word. Reinforce that the **c** spelling is most likely before **i**, **e** and **y**.

(PRACTISE) **Spelling 5, page 16; 'Additional word list'**

(APPLY) Spelling sentences

(ASSESS) Dictation: **The <u>recent</u> <u>incident</u> <u>forced</u> the <u>council</u> to stop further <u>celebrations</u> because of <u>concerns</u> for safety.**

Spelling 5   page 17

(FOCUS) Spelling patterns **ci**, **cu** and **cc**

(TEACH) ▶ Explain that when the letter **c** is combined with other letters it can represent a range of sounds. Write words to illustrate this (for example, **rescue**, **access**, **special**, **vicious**, **magician**). ▶ Discuss the sounds represented by **c** in these words (**rescue**: cue = q), (**access**: acc = x) and 'shun', 'shus' and 'shul' endings. ▶ Explain that it is other letters combined with **c** that create the sounds (for example, **ci** in **cious**, **cial** and **cian** endings). Ask pupils to write other examples with these sounds and spellings (for example, **accident**, **delicious**).

(PRACTISE) **Spelling 5, page 17; 'Additional word list'**

(APPLY) Spelling sentences; independent writing

(ASSESS) Dictation: **Although it seems <u>suspicious</u>, <u>accidents</u> can occur and it may not have been <u>malicious</u> or <u>vicious</u>.**

Spelling 5   page 18

(FOCUS) Words with soft **g**

(TEACH) ▶ Recap when the **c** spelling of a 's' sound occurs (for example, usually before **i**, **e** and **y**). ▶ Discuss if there is a similar pattern for 'j' sounds spelt **g** (soft **g**). ▶ Ask pupils to suggest examples of words containing a soft **g** at the start or in the middle of words, to test the pattern. ▶ Use dictionaries to continue testing the pattern and to find exceptions (for example, **jingle**, **subject**). ▶ Establish that a 'j' sound is often, but not always, spelt **g** before **e**, **i** and **y**, while a 'j' sound before **a**, **o** and **u** will always be spelt **j**.

(PRACTISE) **Spelling 5, page 18; 'Additional word list'**

(APPLY) Spelling sentences

(ASSESS) Dictation: **I <u>imagine</u> it was a <u>genuine</u> and <u>generous</u> <u>gesture</u> from the special <u>agent</u>.**

Spelling 5   page 19

(FOCUS) Silent letters

(TEACH) ▶ Ask pupils to write and show: **wreck**, **knack**, **gnarled**, **ghost**, **listen**, **crumb**. ▶ Check spellings. Recap familiar silent letters (unsounded consonants), for example, **wr**, **kn**, **gn**, **mb**. ▶ On the board, write the words **autum<u>n</u>**, **dou<u>b</u>t**, **s<u>c</u>ene**, **i<u>s</u>land**. Identify the hidden consonants in these words. ▶ Discuss other words with these spelling patterns (for example, **column**, **debt**). ▶ As these spellings cannot be predicted from their sounds, ask pupils to suggest strategies for remembering the silent letters, for example: say it as it's spelt (pronouncing the silent letter); making up mnemonics (for example: scene – scary scene; island – is land).

(PRACTISE) **Spelling 5, page 19; 'Word collector'**

(APPLY) Spelling sentences

(ASSESS) Dictation: **I <u>doubt</u> if the <u>campaign</u> to save the <u>condemned</u> <u>columns</u> will be successful.**

Spelling 5   page 20

FOCUS Words ending **ti** and **tu**

TEACH ▶ Ask pupils to write and show: **vicious, official, musician.** ▶ Check spellings. Recap **cious, cial** and **cian** endings (where **ci** makes a 'sh' sound). ▶ Explain that the same effect occurs with letter **t.** ▶ Say and write: **ambitious, partial, attention.** In colour, write over the 'sh' endings **tion, tial, tious.** ▶ Explain that **ti** or **ci** can usually be distinguished by thinking about the root word (for example: **grace** – gra**ci**ous; **infect** – infec**ti**ous). ▶ Recap 'ch' endings where **tu** makes a 'ch' sound (for example, **picture**). ▶ Show that a similar effect occurs with words ending **tual** (for example, **actual**).

PRACTISE Spelling 5, page 20; 'Spelling log'

APPLY Spelling sentences

ASSESS Dictation: **She made a <u>patient</u> and <u>cautious</u> start, knowing it was <u>essential</u> to get a <u>substantial</u> score.**

Spelling 5   page 21

FOCUS Topic words 2

TEACH ▶ Select a term from current work in science or another subject area (for example, **carbohydrate, oxygen**). Write it on the board. ▶ Ask pupils to take the word apart to make it easier to spell (for example, **car/bo/<u>hy</u>/drate, ox-y-gen**). ▶ Show how to apply spelling knowledge to these words (for example: **y** as a vowel; **g** spelling of 'j' sound before **e**; any roots or suffixes). ▶ Discuss tricky parts (for example, unstressed letters, unusual spelling patterns) and memory strategies to help remember the correct spelling. ▶ Let pupils choose a strategy and use it to practise writing the word.

PRACTISE Spelling 5, page 21; 'Words to practise: My topic words'

APPLY Set mini-target; independent writing in subject area

ASSESS Dictation: **The <u>thermometer</u> will measure the <u>temperature</u> inside the <u>vessel</u>.**

Spelling 5   page 22

FOCUS Prefixes **in, im, ir** and **il**

TEACH ▶ List familiar prefixes for forming opposites (for example, **un, dis, mis, in**). ▶ Say a word and ask pupils to write and show the opposite (for example, **agreeable, tidy, behave, visible**). ▶ Add **ir, il** and **im** to the list. Explain that these are all forms of the **in** prefix. ▶ Write **precise** on the board. Discuss which prefix will make the opposite. Add **im** using a different colour. ▶ Repeat with **(ir)responsible, (il)legible, (im)mobile.** ▶ Establish that a double letter results when **il** is added to a word starting **l**, **ir** is added to a word starting **r** or **im** is added to a word starting **m** (but not if added to words starting **p**).

PRACTISE Spelling 5, page 22; 'Additional word list'

APPLY Spelling sentences

ASSESS Dictation: **He is the most <u>impatient</u>, <u>impolite</u>, <u>irresponsible</u>, <u>incapable</u> and <u>insincere</u> person I know.**

Spelling 5   page 23

FOCUS More **ad** prefixes

TEACH ▶ Ask pupils to write and show: **altogether, although, adverb, admire, adjust.** ▶ Check spellings. Recap prefixes **al** and **ad.** ▶ Explain that **ad**, like the prefix **in**, changes to fit with different letters at the start of root words. ▶ Write **affix**. Ask pupils to identify the prefix and the root (**af/fix**). Repeat with **ap/pear** and **at/tend**. ▶ Write over the prefixes in colour to show that the double letter occurs because the prefix ends with the same letter as the root word starts with. ▶ Contrast this with **a/drift** and **a/float**. Show that the prefix is **a** so there is no double letter.

PRACTISE Spelling 5, page 23; 'Word collector'

APPLY Spelling sentences

ASSESS Dictation: **The police <u>arrived</u> at the <u>address</u> and <u>attempted</u> to <u>apprehend</u> the suspect.**

Spelling 5   page 24

FOCUS Detecting prefixes and roots

TEACH ▶ Ask pupils to write and show familiar prefixes. ▶ Check lists. Recap prefix meanings (for example, **pre** – before; **re** – again; **ex** – out of). ▶ On the board, write **proceed**. Ask pupils to identify the prefix (**pro**). Write over it in colour to show clearly the prefix and root (**pro/ceed**). ▶ Explain that prefixes are not just added to recognisable root words – **ceed** is the original root. ▶ Swap **pro** for prefix **suc** to form the word **succeed**, from the same root. ▶ Repeat with **per/mit** and **sub/mit**. ▶ Add new prefixes to the list (for example, **per, pro, suc, sub**).

PRACTISE **Spelling 5**, page 24; 'Spelling log' or 'Word collector'

APPLY Independent writing

ASSESS Dictation: **I <u>prefer</u> to <u>support</u> local shops, <u>providing</u> they <u>supply</u> <u>perfect</u> <u>produce</u>.**

Spelling 5   page 25

FOCUS Homophones

TEACH ▶ Without giving any context, say homophones for pupils to write (for example, **court, pier, cereal**). ▶ Prompt discussion about homophones and the importance of context when spelling them (need to know the meaning to choose the correct spellings). ▶ Clarify the word required (for example: *I meant law* **court**/*seaside* **pier**/*breakfast* **cereal**.) and then check spellings. ▶ Ask pupils to write the homophone for each word. ▶ Discuss the contexts in which each homophone might be used, for example: **pier** if writing about a seaside location (specific use); **peer** as a synonym for 'look' (more general use).

PRACTISE **Spelling 5**, page 25; 'Additional word list'

APPLY Spelling sentences or independent writing

ASSESS Dictation: **I <u>guessed</u> we <u>would</u> <u>need</u> to <u>alter</u> the <u>route</u> to the summer <u>fete</u>.**

Spelling 5   page 26

FOCUS Revision 2

TEACH ▶ Use this session to focus on a spelling problem you have noticed from analysing pupils' independent writing. ▶ Revise the guideline, rule, pattern or strategy that has not been fully grasped to help avoid the same error in future. ▶ Set a relevant target for all independent writing and proof reading to focus attention on applying the learning.

PRACTISE **Spelling 5**, page 26; previous 'Additional word lists' (select as appropriate)

APPLY Independent writing; proof reading; respond to marking

ASSESS Paired testing; independent writing

Spelling 5   page 27

FOCUS Topic words 3

TEACH ▶ Select a term related to your current work in maths (for example, **digital, approximately**). Write it on the board. ▶ Ask pupils to explain how they will take it apart. Encourage them to use word structure as well as syllables (for example, **digit/al**) and discuss how this strategy helps to spell the word. ▶ Discuss features that might make the word difficult, and memory strategies to overcome them. ▶ Cover the word and ask pupils to write it using the strategies.

PRACTISE **Spelling 5**, page 27; 'Words to practise: My topic words'

APPLY Set mini-target; independent writing

ASSESS Dictation: **I estimate it must weigh approximately forty kilograms.**

Spelling 5 — page 28

FOCUS Adding suffixes: words ending **e**

TEACH ▶ Display two lists of suffixes: vowel suffixes (for example, **ed**, **ing**, **er**) and consonant suffixes (for example, **ly**, **ful**, **less**). ▶ Write words ending with **e** (for example, **hope**, **hate**, **live**). Ask pupils to add suffixes to these words. ▶ Check spellings and confirm the main rule: drop the **e** to add vowel suffixes; retain the **e** to add consonant suffixes. ▶ Use the rule with other vowel suffixes (for example, **latish**, **driven**). ▶ Write the word **die**. Discuss adding **ing**. Establish that if a word ends **ie**, the **ie** changes to **y** to avoid double **i** (**dying**).

PRACTISE Spelling 5, page 28; 'Additional word list'; 'Word sort 1'

APPLY Set target; independent writing

ASSESS Dictation: **It was extremely difficult, but she refused to give in and achieved the required standard.**

Spelling 5 — page 29

FOCUS Adding suffixes: words ending **y**

TEACH ▶ Display the list of vowel and consonant suffixes used previously. ▶ Write words ending with **y** (for example, **lazy**, **happy**, **empty**, **enjoy**). Ask pupils to add suffixes to the words. ▶ Check spellings and confirm the main rule: if a word ends consonant **y**, change **y** to **i** for all suffixes except **ing** (with **ing**, retain **y** to avoid double **i**). ▶ Write the word **shy** and then **shied**, **shyly**, **shyness**. Explain that short one-syllable words like this are an exception to the main rule.

PRACTISE Spelling 5, page 29; 'Word sort 1'

APPLY Add to targets; independent writing

ASSESS Dictation: **The terrified people scurried for shelter carrying their supplies.**

Spelling 5 — page 30

FOCUS Adding suffixes: double the last letter

TEACH ▶ Ask pupils to write and show: **admitted, worshipped, forgotten**. ▶ Check spellings. Revise the main rule for doubling consonants when adding vowel suffixes. ▶ Write **picnic** and **picnicking**. Discuss how the root word changes. ▶ Establish that two-syllable words ending **c** add **k** to form the double consonant. ▶ Ask pupils to write **panicked**. ▶ Write **target** and **targeting**. Discuss why **t** is not doubled. ▶ Explain that the final consonant is not doubled if that syllable is unstressed (i.e. you say tar/**get** not **tar**/get). ▶ Ask pupils to write **limiting** and **limited**.

PRACTISE Spelling 5, page 30; 'Additional word list'

APPLY Set target; independent writing

ASSESS Dictation: **He is admitting that his horse panicked and went galloping through the picnickers.**

Spelling 5 — page 31

FOCUS Words ending **ous**

TEACH ▶ Ask pupils to write and show: **famous, nervous, furious, envious, marvellous**. ▶ Check spellings. Discuss root words and spelling changes. ▶ Establish that the usual rules for adding suffixes apply when adding **ous** (drop **e**; **y** to **i**; double last letter). ▶ Explain that sometimes other changes are required to add **ous**. Write **vigour** and **vigorous**. Discuss the change. ▶ Establish that words ending **our** drop the **u**. ▶ Repeat with **courage**/**courageous**. ▶ Explain that words ending with soft **ce** or soft **ge** keep the **e** to keep the sound soft. ▶ Tell pupils to look out for other exceptions to the main rules when adding **ous**.

PRACTISE Spelling 5, page 31; 'Additional word list'

APPLY Spelling sentences

ASSESS Dictation: **Curiously, a humorous and marvellous story came out of a disastrous event.**

Spelling 5   page 32

FOCUS Words ending **able** and **ible**

TEACH ▶ Ask pupils to write and show: **forgivable, adorable, reliable, sensible, reversible**. ▶ Check spellings. Recap **able** and **ible** endings (for example, **ible** after letter **s**). ▶ Discuss the root words and spelling change when the suffix is added. ▶ Establish that the main rules for adding suffixes apply when adding **able** or **ible**.

On the board, write **replace** and then **replaceable**. Discuss the spelling change. ▶ Establish that words ending soft **ce** or **ge** keep the **e** when **able** is added, in order to keep the soft **c**. ▶ Ask pupils to write **chargeable**.

PRACTISE **Spelling 5**, page 32; 'Additional word list'

APPLY Spelling sentences

ASSESS Dictation: **It was <u>noticeable</u> that the weather was more <u>changeable</u> and less <u>reliable</u>.**

Spelling 5   page 33

FOCUS Topic words 4

TEACH ▶ Select one or two terms relating to your current literacy work (for example, **simile, onomatopoeia**). Write them on the board. ▶ Invite pupils to explain how to take the word apart to identify the tricky parts. Explain that even the most difficult word is easier to spell once it is broken down (for example, **on/o/ma/to/poe/ia**). ▶ Identify tricky parts and decide on memory tricks for them (for example: chant letter names (p-o-e-i-a); **poe** like **poem**). ▶ Cover the word and ask pupils to write it using the strategies.

PRACTISE **Spelling 5**, page 33; 'Words to practise: My topic words'

APPLY Set mini-target; independent writing

ASSESS Dictation: **The speaker used <u>repetition</u>, <u>rhetorical</u> <u>questions</u> and powerful <u>imagery</u> in her <u>argument</u>.**

Spelling 5   page 34

FOCUS Word structure

TEACH ▶ Revise the idea that many words are built from root words and affixes. Give a root word (for example, **place**). ▶ Ask pupils to build as many words as they can by adding affixes to it (for example, **replacement, irreplaceable, misplaced**). ▶ Collect examples on the board, reinforcing guidelines and rules for adding suffixes. ▶ On the board, write **depression** and **recreation**. ▶ Discuss how understanding word structure (root words and affixes) can help to spell these words correctly (for example: recognising affixes and roots; building up words from the parts).

PRACTISE **Spelling 5**, page 34; 'Spelling log'

APPLY Set target; independent writing across subject areas

ASSESS Dictation: **There was general <u>disapproval</u> when the <u>recreation</u> ground was closed.**

Spelling 5   page 35

FOCUS Word families

TEACH ▶ Recap word families (words with a shared root, linked by meaning). ▶ Ask pupils to write and show words related to **quest**. ▶ Repeat with **please**. ▶ Collect the words on the board, looking for shared spellings. ▶ On the board, write **medic, medical, medicate, medicine**. Discuss how knowing this word family helps to spell **medicine**. ▶ Establish that thinking about word roots and linked family words is another useful strategy in spelling words.

PRACTISE **Spelling 5**, page 35; 'Spelling log'

APPLY Spelling sentences

ASSESS Dictation: **The <u>majority</u> <u>realise</u> that having a <u>variety</u> of <u>designs</u> is a <u>definite</u> <u>improvement</u>.**

Spelling 5   page 36

FOCUS Word histories

TEACH ▶ Recap familiar Greek and Latin roots. Ask pupils to write and show words with the root **tele** (for example, **telephone**, **television**, **telescope**). Check spellings. Revise the meaning of **tele** (far). ▶ On the board, write **auto**. Ask pupils to use a dictionary to find words starting with this Greek prefix. ▶ Write examples on the board, discussing meaning and structure (for example, **auto mat ic**). ▶ Establish the meaning of **auto** (self). ▶ Cover one or two of the words and ask pupils to write them. ▶ Discuss how knowing about the roots and word origins can help to spell words.

PRACTISE **Spelling 5**, page 36; 'Additional word list'

APPLY Spelling sentences

ASSESS Dictation: **Can we** interrupt **your** interview **to take a** photograph **outside the** aquatic **centre?**

Spelling 5   page 37

FOCUS Common confusions

TEACH ▶ Ask pupils to write and show: It was **quite quiet**. ▶ Check spellings. Explain that **quite** and **quiet** are sometimes confused because they have similar spellings, although they sound different. ▶ Repeat with **wary** and **weary**. Write the words on the board so pupils can check their spelling. ▶ Discuss strategies to help distinguish these words (for example: the 'ear' sound and spelling in **weary**; be **wary** if you are **weary**). ▶ Ask pupils for other words that they mix up (for example: **loose**, **lose**; **desert**, **dessert**). ▶ Discuss strategies for making the right choice.

PRACTISE **Spelling 5**, page 37; 'Spelling log'

APPLY Spelling sentences; independent writing

ASSESS Dictation: **Be** wary **of** loose **chippings if you** choose **to** proceed**.**

Spelling 5   page 38

FOCUS Revision 3

TEACH ▶ Use this session to reinforce rules for adding suffixes. ▶ Focus on rules pupils are having problems with applying. ▶ Give each pair of pupils a 'Word sort 1' grid with columns headed with guidelines (for example: 'drop the **e**' and 'keep the **e**' or 'double' and 'don't double'). Say a word (for example, **recreating**). Ask pupils, in pairs, to decide which rule applies and to write the word in the right column. In pairs, check spellings and reinforce rules.

PRACTISE **Spelling 5**, page 38; previous 'Additional word lists'; 'Word sort 1'

APPLY Proof reading; respond to marking; check targets

ASSESS Through independent writing

Spelling 5   page 39

FOCUS Personal spelling list

TEACH ▶ Display a copy of the 'Words to practise: My tricky words'. Explain that good spellers learn to monitor their own spelling. A blank grid like this can be used to record words that they often have difficulty with and then learn to spell them correctly. ▶ Recap the process of taking the word apart and then identifying the tricky part(s) that trip up pupils when writing it. ▶ Give out copies of 'Learning and practising tricky words' (1 or 2, as appropriate) to remind them of useful strategies for remembering the correct spelling.

PRACTISE **Spelling 5**, page 39; 'Words to practise: My tricky words'; 'Learning and practising tricky words'

APPLY Set own mini-target; independent writing

ASSESS Pupils work in pairs to compose dictation sentences to test each other on chosen words.

Spelling 6

Spelling 6　　　　　　　　　　　　page 4

FOCUS Representing sounds

TEACH ▶ Recap sound spelling strategies of breaking words into syllables and phonemes. ▶ Ask pupils to write and show: **electric**, **wicket**, **skittle**, **unique**, **chorus**. ▶ Check spellings. Recap the alternative spellings of the 'k' sound in these words. ▶ Explain that many sounds like 'k' can be spelt in alternative ways, so a good speller must know when to use the more unusual spellings. ▶ Discuss 'k' spelling patterns (for example: **ic** and **que** at the end; **ch** in classical Greek words).

Discuss other vowel and consonant sounds with alternative spellings (for example: 'sh' in **machine**; 'i' in **syllable**).

PRACTISE Spelling 6, page 4; 'Word collector' or 'Spelling log'

APPLY Set target; independent writing

ASSESS Dictation: **I <u>guarantee</u> there will be <u>chaos</u> when the <u>celebrity guest</u> unveils the statue.**

Spelling 6　　　　　　　　　　　　page 5

FOCUS Building words with affixes

TEACH ▶ Ask pupils to write and show: **mistaken**, **immobile**, **disinterested**, **unhurried**, **changeable**. ▶ Check spellings. Discuss strategies used and how the structure of words (roots, prefixes and suffixes) helps to spell words. ▶ Recap rules for adding affixes (for example: drop **e** to add vowel suffixes, but also exceptions, like **changeable**; changing **y** to **i**; just add prefix). ▶ Model writing words with multiple affixes (for example, **effect/ive/ness**, **doubt/ful/ly**) by saying and spelling each part of the word in turn. ▶ Establish that the same spelling rules apply when adding affix to affix.

PRACTISE Spelling 6, page 5; 'Additional word list'

APPLY Add to targets; independent writing

ASSESS Dictation: **<u>Undoubtedly</u>, he is <u>irreplaceable</u> and there is some <u>uneasiness</u> about the future of the <u>restoration</u>.**

Spelling 6　　　　　　　　　　　　page 6

FOCUS Rules and exceptions

TEACH ▶ Ask pupils to write and show: **directly**, **lovely**, **lonely**, **really**, **tidily**, **simply**, **hopefully**. ▶ Check spellings. Recap the main rules for adding **ly** (just add **ly**; keep final **e**; change **y** to **i**). ▶ Clarify the exception for words ending **le** (drop the **le**, add **ly**). Write the word **comfortably** on the board to demonstrate that this extends to words ending **able** and **ible**. ▶ Introduce further exceptions, for example, words ending **ic** (**basic** – **basic<u>ally</u>**) and tricky short words (for example, **true** – **truly**). ▶ Explain that it is important to know exceptions as well as the main rules.

PRACTISE Spelling 6, page 6; 'Additional word list'

APPLY Add to targets; independent writing

ASSESS Dictation: **<u>Fortunately</u>, there is still the <u>possibility</u> that they might <u>actually</u> complete the job <u>successfully</u>.**

Spelling 6　　　　　　　　　　　　page 7

FOCUS Word relationships

TEACH ▶ Ask pupils to write and show: **definite**, **pleasure**, **knowledge**, **medicine**. ▶ Check spellings. Recap how thinking about related words helps to spell these words (for example: revealing hidden letters (**know/ledge**); clarifying spelling of ambiguous sounds (**medic/ine**); making unstressed vowels clear (**define/ definite**)). ▶ Discuss an example where a longer word helps to spell a shorter root word (for example, **sign** – **signature**). ▶ Explain that silent letters are sometimes sounded in linked longer words (for example, **debt/debit**).

PRACTISE Spelling 6, page 7; 'Word collector'

APPLY Add to targets; independent writing

ASSESS Dictation: **More <u>resources</u> are needed to <u>ensure</u> a complete <u>transformation</u> of the <u>design</u> for the <u>reservoir</u>.**

Spelling 6 — page 8

FOCUS Visual strategies

TEACH ▶ Ask pupils to write and show: **honour, height, relief, thorough.** ▶ Check spellings. Recap that sound strategies alone are not always reliable. ▶ Demonstrate how visual strategies can help spell these words, for example, looking for words within words (**lie** in r**elie**f; **our** in hon**our**). ▶ Make up mnemonics/memory tricks to support the visual strategies (for example: to **lie** down is a r**elie**f; on **our** hon**our**).

PRACTISE **Spelling 6**, page 8; 'Word collector' or 'Spelling log'

APPLY Independent writing

ASSESS Dictation: **I thoroughly enjoyed the journey to a foreign country, apart from the savage climate.**

Spelling 6 — page 9

FOCUS Tricky words 1

TEACH ▶ Select connectives or adverbs that would be useful in current writing. Write an example on the board, such as **alternatively.** ▶ Explain that in longer connectives the vowels are sometimes slurred. ▶ Model how to take the word apart or build it up, starting with the root word and adding each suffix in turn: **alter – alternate – alternative – alternatively.** ▶ Reinforce the rules for keeping or dropping the **e** as you go. ▶ Ask pupils to write the word as you say the stages. ▶ Discuss other strategies to check the spelling (for example, *Can you see the words* **alter** *and* **native**?).

PRACTISE **Spelling 6**, page 9; 'Words to practise: My tricky words'

APPLY Set mini-target; independent writing; proof reading

ASSESS Dictation: **Originally, an easy victory was expected, but the result was contrary to all expectations.**

Spelling 6 — page 10

FOCUS Unstressed vowels

TEACH ▶ Ask pupils to write and show: **different, miserable, family, vegetable, chocolate.** ▶ Check spellings. Recap difficulties caused by unstressed vowels or syllables. ▶ Recap useful strategies, for example: say all the syllables clearly, including the unstressed part (dif-**fer**-ent); use exaggerated pronunciation (choc-**o**-late); think of root words and affixes (**miser**-able). ▶ Write words with more than one unstressed vowel (for example, **category, temperature**). Discuss strategies for writing and remembering them.

PRACTISE **Spelling 6**, page 10; 'Additional word list'

APPLY Set target; independent writing

ASSESS Dictation: **After several months in development, it was a memorable day when the laboratory finally opened for business.**

Spelling 6 — page 11

FOCUS Unstressed consonants

TEACH ▶ Ask pupils to write and show: **Wednesday, February.** ▶ Check spellings. Identify the tricky unstressed consonants and discuss the strategies pupils used (for example: saying the syllables; emphasising the hidden part – Feb-**ru**-ary). ▶ Write **government**. Say it normally (gover-ment). Invite pupils to identify the unstressed **n**. ▶ Discuss strategies to make the spelling clear, for example, find the root word (**govern**). ▶ Repeat with **handbag**. ▶ Explain that the consonants are lost as words are built up, so taking them apart helps reveal them.

PRACTISE **Spelling 6**, page 11; 'Spelling log'

APPLY Spelling sentences

ASSESS Dictation: **On Wednesday the twelfth of February local government has organised an exhibition about the environment.**

Spelling 6   page 12

FOCUS Unstressed endings: ant, ance, ent, ence

TEACH ▶ Ask pupils to write and show: **confident**, **confidence**, **important**, **importance**. ▶ Check spellings. Establish that **ant** words use **ance**; **ent** use **ence**. ▶ Discuss problems with distinguishing between **ent** and **ant** (or **ence** and **ance**) in normal speech. ▶ Explain that sometimes it can help to think of related words where the **a** or **e** sound is more clear (for example, confid**e**ntial). ▶ Another guideline is that **ence** usually follows soft **g** or **c** to keep the sound soft (for example, ag**e**nt). ▶ A useful technique for remembering the correct spelling is to stress the ending (for example, import**ant**).

PRACTISE **Spelling 6**, page 12; 'Additional word list'; 'Word sort 3'

APPLY Spelling sentences or independent writing

ASSESS Dictation: **I am <u>confident</u> that there will be no <u>significant</u> <u>disturbance</u> during the <u>president's</u> visit.**

Spelling 6   page 13

FOCUS Double or single consonants

TEACH ▶ Ask pupils to write and show: **misspell**, **riddle**, **disappoint**. ▶ Check spellings. Explain that a common problem is whether to use double or single consonants. ▶ Discuss reasons for double letters in the words they have just written (for example: a prefix that ends with the same letter the root word starts with; keeping a short vowel short). ▶ Establish that in most cases there is a reason for the double consonants. ▶ Demonstrate that in a few tricky words a mnemonic or memory trick can help (for example, **necessary** – one **c**ollar and two **s**leeves).

PRACTISE **Spelling 6**, page 13; 'Additional word list'

APPLY Spelling sentences

ASSESS Dictation: **I would be too <u>embarrassed</u> to <u>recommend</u> this <u>dismal</u> <u>accommodation</u>.**

Spelling 6   page 14

FOCUS Revision 1

TEACH ▶ Use this session to focus on word endings that are causing difficulties in pupils' writing. ▶ Write up some examples and discuss the cause of the problem (for example: Is the ending not spelt as it sounds (**ture**)? Is it unstressed (**ant**, **ent**)? Is there a choice (**tion**, **cian**, **sion**)?). ▶ Reinforce helpful strategies and guidelines for correcting the spellings and remembering them in the future.

PRACTISE **Spelling 6**, page 14; 'Spelling log'

APPLY Proof reading; respond to marking; check targets

ASSESS Through independent writing

Spelling 6   page 15

FOCUS Tricky words 2

TEACH ▶ Select two foreign imports to write on the board (for example, **pyjamas** and **yacht**). ▶ Explain that these words have unusual spelling patterns because they are originally from another language (**pyjamas** from Hindi and **yacht** from Dutch). ▶ Demonstrate that it is still possible to take the words apart to identify the tricky part (for example: **py/ja/mas**; **y/ach/t**). ▶ Discuss strategies to remember the words, for example: analogy (**py** like in **py**lon); mnemonics (look for **jam** in your **pyjamas**).

PRACTISE **Spelling 6**, page 15; 'Words to practise: My tricky words'

APPLY Spelling sentences

ASSESS Dictation: **The <u>amateur</u> artist made <u>silhouettes</u> of the tropical islands to sell as holiday <u>souvenirs</u>.**

Spelling 6   page 16

FOCUS Prefixes to support spelling

TEACH ▶ Ask pupils to write a list of prefixes with examples of words that include them. ▶ Check spellings. Recap that prefixes change meaning but not spelling. ▶ Give a root or root word (for example, **form**). Discuss how many prefixes can be attached to make different words (for example, **inform, deform, perform, conform, transform**). Use the words in sentences to revise how the meanings are changed. ▶ Ask pupils, in pairs, to repeat the exercise by swapping the prefix on another word, for example, **subject** (**inject, project**).

PRACTISE **Spelling 6**, page 16; 'Additional word list'

APPLY Set target; independent writing

ASSESS Dictation: **If you <u>persevere</u> you might <u>exceed</u> your own <u>expectations</u> and <u>attain</u> great things.**

Spelling 6   page 17

FOCUS Choosing the correct prefix

TEACH ▶ Ask pupils to write and show: **immoral, invisible, enjoy, unsure, equip**. ▶ Check spellings, revising prefixes **in, im, un, en, e**. ▶ On the board, write: **inprison, inlarge, emense**. Ask pupils to spot where the error occurs in each word (i.e. the wrong prefix). ▶ Discuss why errors like this might occur (for example, the prefixes sound similar when words are pronounced normally). ▶ Write the correct spellings (**imprison, enlarge, immense**). ▶ Reinforce that understanding and knowing more about prefixes helps use the right one (for example, **im** rather than **in** before the letter **p**).

PRACTISE **Spelling 6**, page 17; 'Word collector'

APPLY Spelling sentences

ASSESS Dictation: **She had to <u>endure</u> <u>imprisonment</u> although convinced it was an <u>injustice</u>.**

Spelling 6   page 18

FOCUS Hyphens

TEACH ▶ Pupils will be familiar with hyphens from reading. Discuss their purpose (to join two words or a prefix to a word). ▶ Explain that a hyphen is only used if needed. ▶ Write on the board **cowriter** and **co-writer**. Discuss why the hyphen is needed (to avoid a confusing clash of letter). ▶ Repeat with **coown** and **co-own**. Here the hyphen is needed because the prefix ends and root word begins with a vowel. ▶ Ask pupils to look for other uses of hyphens, for example, joining prefixes to words starting with a capital letter (**pro-Europe**) or to avoid confusing word combinations.

PRACTISE **Spelling 6**, page 18; 'Additional word list'

APPLY Spelling sentences or independent writing

ASSESS Dictation: **The <u>co-owner</u> resigned but was later <u>re-elected</u>.**

Spelling 6   page 19

FOCUS Common confusions 1

TEACH ▶ On the board, write **advice** and **advise**. Establish the correct pronunciation for each (**advice** rhymes with **nice**; **advise** rhymes with **wise**). ▶ Discuss why they are confused (similar sound, spelling and meanings). ▶ Use the words in sentences to establish their meaning and identify the noun and the verb (for example, **Take my <u>advice</u>.** (noun) **I <u>advise</u> you to go.** (verb)). Discuss strategies for remembering which is which, for example, using the sound (**nice** to have **advice**; must be **wise** to **advise**). ▶ Explain the pattern **se** for verbs, **ce** for noun. This can be used to distinguish between other words, such as **practice** and **practise**.

PRACTISE **Spelling 6**, page 19; 'Word sort 1'

APPLY Spelling sentences; respond to marking

ASSESS Dictation: **I believe you should take my <u>advice</u> and put it into <u>practice</u>.**

Spelling 6	page 20

FOCUS Homophones and near homophones

TEACH ▶ Select a pair of homophones that pupils are getting confused (for example, **accept/except**, **current/currant**). *Note:* **Accept** and **except** are not true homophones, but as the first syllable is often unstressed they sound alike. ▶ Establish the meaning of each word and orally devise sentences using each word correctly. ▶ Discuss strategies for remembering the correct word, for example, using related words (**accept – acceptable**; **except – exception**; **stationery** – comes from the **stationer**).

PRACTISE Spelling 6, page 20; 'Additional word list'

APPLY Spelling sentences; proof reading

ASSESS Dictation: I <u>accept</u> there was a <u>minor</u> problem in the <u>past</u> but <u>currently</u> we are on course.

Spelling 6	page 21

FOCUS Topic words 1

TEACH ▶ Select one or two words related to your current work in another subject area. Write the words on the board. ▶ Ask pupils, in pairs, to take the word apart and identify the tricky parts. Invite feedback, encouraging pupils to explain how they have taken the word apart and which tricky bits they have found. ▶ Discuss helpful strategies for remembering the spelling. ▶ Cover the word and ask pupils to write it using the strategies.

PRACTISE Spelling 6, page 21; 'Words to practise: My topic words'

APPLY Set mini-target; independent writing; respond to marking

ASSESS Dictation: <u>Contemporary</u> documents show that child poverty was an important <u>issue</u> in Victorian <u>society</u>.

Spelling 6	page 22

FOCUS Adding suffixes to words ending **l**

TEACH ▶ Ask pupils to write and show: **forgetting**, **forbidden**, **limited**. ▶ Check spellings. Recap that the consonant is doubled if the syllable is stressed; not doubled if the syllable is unstressed. ▶ On the board, write: **traveller**, **travelled**, **travelling**. Establish that if a word ends with a vowel and **l**, the **l** is always doubled before adding vowel suffixes such as **ing**, **ed**, **er** and **en**. ▶ Write **equal**. Ask pupils to follow the pattern to write **equalled** and **equalling**. ▶ Explain that the rule does not apply to some suffixes, such as **ity** and **ise**. ▶ Ask pupils to write **equality**.

PRACTISE Spelling 6, page 22; 'Additional word list'

APPLY Set target; independent writing

ASSESS Dictation: They <u>shovelled</u> earth and <u>levelled</u> the ground to hide the <u>tunnelling</u>.

Spelling 6	page 23

FOCUS Adding suffixes to words ending **fer**

TEACH ▶ Ask pupils to write and show: **traveller**, **woollen**, **channelled**, **excellence**. ▶ Check spellings, reinforcing that **l** is always doubled when adding these suffixes. ▶ On the board, write **refer**. Demonstrate adding suffixes: **referred**, **referring**, **referee**, **reference**. ▶ Discuss why the **r** is doubled in the first two but not the second two. ▶ Establish that the **r** is doubled if the **fer** is still stressed once the suffix is added but not if the **fer** becomes unstressed (i.e. the stress moves to the first part of the word, **ref**). ▶ Ask pupils to follow the pattern to write **preferred** and **preference**.

PRACTISE Spelling 6, page 23; 'Word sort 1'

APPLY Independent writing or spelling sentences

ASSESS Dictation: Being <u>transferred</u> to a <u>different</u> team would be my <u>preference</u>.

Spelling 6 page 24

FOCUS Adding **ate**, **ify**, **ise** and **en**

TEACH ▶ List suffixes used to change words into verbs: **ate**, **ify**, **en**, **ise**. ▶ Ask pupils to write and show the words **active**, **simple**, **wide**, **energy**, **real** and the verbs formed from them. ▶ Check spellings, recapping the usual changes when adding vowel suffixes (for example: drop the **e**; **y** to **i**). ▶ Recap that **l** does not double when adding **ise**. ▶ Write the word **vapour** and the verbs **vaporise** and **evaporate**. Discuss the change in the spelling. ▶ Establish that sometimes there are other spelling changes when these suffixes are added. ▶ Ask pupils to write **vapour**, **vaporise** and **evaporate**.

PRACTISE **Spelling 6**, page 24; 'Word sort 3'

APPLY Spelling sentences

ASSESS Dictation: **Mr James was horrified that the plans were modified without notifying him first.**

Spelling 6 page 25

FOCUS Changes to root words

TEACH ▶ Ask pupils to write and show the words **severe**, **empty**, **exclude**, **local** and then nouns formed from them (**severity**, **emptiness**, **exclusion**, **locality**). ▶ Check spellings. Revise familiar rules for adding the suffixes. ▶ On the board, write **possible** and **possibility**, **able** and **ability**. Discuss the change in spelling. ▶ Establish that when adding **ity** to words ending **ible/able**, **le** is dropped and **ility** added. Demonstrate that the pronunciation helps signal the change (for example, **pos/si/bil/ity**). ▶ Establish that other root words also change when these suffixes are added, for example, **curious** – **curiosity** (words ending **our/ous** drop the **u** when **ity** is added).

PRACTISE **Spelling 6**, page 25; 'Additional word list'

APPLY Spelling sentences

ASSESS Dictation: **The sports personality thanked the crowd for their generosity on a variety of occasions.**

Spelling 6 page 26

FOCUS Revision 2

TEACH ▶ Use this opportunity to focus on words with affixes that are causing problems in independent writing. ▶ Write examples on the board and demonstrate checking each part of the word in turn (prefix, root, suffix). ▶ Classify the problems, for example: incorrect spelling of a prefix/suffix (**regardles**, **inforce**); mistake with adding the prefix/suffix (**unsteadyness**, **imensely**); error in the root word. ▶ Reinforce the rules or understanding required to correct the errors and ensure they are not repeated.

PRACTISE **Spelling 6**, page 26; 'Spelling log'

APPLY Proof reading; respond to marking; check targets

ASSESS Through independent writing

Spelling 6 page 27

FOCUS Topic words 2

TEACH ▶ Select a term from your current work in English. Write it on the board. ▶ Ask pupils, in pairs, to take the word apart and identify the tricky parts. Invite feedback, encouraging pupils to explain how they have taken the word apart (for example: roots and affixes; syllables) and which tricky bits they have found (for example: unusual spelling patterns; unsounded consonants). ▶ Discuss helpful strategies for remembering the correct spelling of the tricky parts (for example, make up a mnemonic for **mnemonic**). ▶ Cover the word and ask pupils to write it using their chosen strategies.

PRACTISE **Spelling 6**, page 27; 'Words to practise: My topic words'

APPLY Set mini-target; independent writing

ASSESS Dictation: **I used a mnemonic to help me learn to spell encyclopaedia and synonym.**

| Spelling 6 | page 28 |

FOCUS Word families

TEACH ▶ Ask pupils to write and show: **bomb**, **bombard**; **know**, **acknowledge**. ▶ Check spellings; revise how using related words helps spell linked words. ▶ Give a root word (for example, **part**). Ask pupils, in pairs, to write a family of words with the same root (for example, **particle**, **particular**, **partition**, **participate**, **impart**). ▶ Invite feedback. Collect words on the board. ▶ Discuss where the link to the word **part** is most helpful (for example, **par**ticular). ▶ Establish that words originally from the same root word share spelling patterns even if they no longer sound alike.

PRACTISE Spelling 6, page 28; 'Word collector'

APPLY Set target; independent writing

ASSESS Dictation: **The secretary did a tremendous impersonation of a well-known television personality.**

| Spelling 6 | page 29 |

FOCUS Latin and Greek roots

TEACH ▶ Ask pupils to write and show: **bicycle**, **unicycle**, **binoculars**; **automobile**, **autocue**. ▶ Check spellings. Recap known Latin and Greek roots. Discuss how this knowledge helped to spell the words (for example, **bi/cycle** clarifies where **i** and **y** go). ▶ Say words with the same root (for example, *inspect*, *spectacles*). Ask pupils to identify the shared root and work out the meaning (**spect** = see). ▶ Ask pupils to write and show the word **spectator**. ▶ Check spelling. Reinforce how recognising the root within a word helps spelling.

PRACTISE Spelling 6, page 29; 'Additional word list'

APPLY Spelling sentences

ASSESS Dictation: **From my perspective, it was incredible how she manipulated the audience.**

| Spelling 6 | page 30 |

FOCUS Formation of words

TEACH ▶ Recap how words are constructed from common roots. Help pupils write word chains, changing one part of the word at a time (for example: **octopus – octagon – heptagon – heptathlon – decathlon – decimal**). ▶ Discuss the meaning of the root parts as you go (for example: **octo** = 8; **gon** = angles; **hepta** = 7). ▶ Ask pupils to write and show other words with the same roots (for example, **hexagon**, **polygon**, **decimetre**, **triathlon**).

PRACTISE Spelling 6, page 30; 'Additional word list'

APPLY Spelling sentences

ASSESS Dictation: **In his biography the astronaut described travelling through the Earth's atmosphere.**

| Spelling 6 | page 31 |

FOCUS Greek spelling patterns

TEACH ▶ Ask pupils to write and show: **photograph**, **telephone**, **phonics**, **technology**. ▶ Check spellings, revising **ph** spelling of 'f' and **ch** spelling of 'k'. Explain that these spelling patterns occur in many words derived from Greek roots, such as **graph**, **photo**, **phon(o)**, **tech**. ▶ Discuss what sort of words have these patterns (for example, more often found in technical words). ▶ Ask pupils to use a dictionary to find words with other Greek patterns, such as **ps** and **phy**.

PRACTISE Spelling 6, page 31; 'Additional word list'

APPLY Spelling sentences

ASSESS Dictation: **The symphony was a triumph for the orchestra, but the hysterical conductor was a physical wreck.**

Spelling 6   page 32

FOCUS Word endings

TEACH ▶ Ask pupils to write and show: **junior**, **million**, **aquarium**, **radius**. ▶ Write the words on the board so pupils can check their spellings. Recap roots and origins. ▶ Write over the word endings (**ior**, **ion**, **ium**, **ius**). Discuss the pronunciation and why this might lead to misspellings (for example, **eon** rather than **ion**). ▶ Ask pupils to write other words with these endings (for example, **rebellion**, **medium**).

PRACTISE Spelling 6, page 32; 'Additional word list'

APPLY Spelling sentences

ASSESS Dictation: **My <u>companion</u> requested <u>superior</u> seats in the <u>auditorium</u> after winning a <u>million</u>.**

Spelling 6   page 33

FOCUS Topic words 3

TEACH ▶ Select a term from your current work in maths (for example, **quadrilateral**, **perpendicular**). Write it on the board. ▶ Recap taking the word apart (breaking it into syllables or root and affixes). Show that much of the word is straightforward once this is done. ▶ Identify tricky parts (for example, unstressed vowels/endings). Discuss helpful strategies including links to related words and Greek or Latin roots (**circular – perpendicular**; **quad**). ▶ Cover the word and ask pupils to write it using the chosen strategies.

PRACTISE Spelling 6, page 33; 'Words to practise: My topic words'

APPLY Set mini-target; independent writing in the subject

ASSESS Dictation: **Do you have a <u>strategy</u> for measuring the <u>perimeter</u> of this <u>quadrilateral</u>?**

Spelling 6   page 34

FOCUS Common confusions 2

TEACH ▶ Ask pupils to write and show: **comical**, **icicle**, **miracle**. ▶ Check spellings, focusing on the different spellings of the 'ic'/'ul' ending. ▶ Discuss strategies for distinguishing between these endings. Establish that **ical** is an adjective ending formed when **al** is added to **ic**; **icle** and **acle** are both noun endings, which can sometimes be distinguished by the sound if the words are pronounced slowly. ▶ An alternative strategy is to think of a linked word where the sound is more clear (for example, **miraculous**).

PRACTISE Spelling 6, page 34; 'Word sort' 1 or 2

APPLY Spelling sentences

ASSESS Dictation: **The parade of <u>vehicles</u> made quite a <u>comical</u> <u>spectacle</u>.**

Spelling 6   page 35

FOCUS Common confusions 3

TEACH ▶ Look in pupils' writing for examples of: joined words that should be separate (for example, **infact** for **in fact**); separate words that should be joined (for example, **where as** for **whereas**); using hyphens unnecessarily (for example, **ex-actly**); mistaking commonly confused words (for example, **all ready** and **already**). ▶ Write an example on the board. Explain the correct usage and invite pupils to compose and write a sentence showing the word or phrase used correctly.

PRACTISE Spelling 6, page 35; 'Spelling log'

APPLY Independent writing; proof reading; respond to marking

ASSESS Dictation: **As <u>always</u>, <u>in spite</u> of the rain, <u>a lot</u> of people were <u>already</u> there.**

Spelling 6   page 36

FOCUS People and places

TEACH ▶ Show a map of the world or use atlases to look at names of countries. Discuss which are easy to spell and which are more difficult. ▶ Ask pupils, in pairs, to identify a tricky example and decide on the tricky part and how they might remember it. ▶ Invite them to share and try out different strategies. ▶ Discuss suffixes, or endings, that appear on words associated with nationality (for example, the **Japanese** flag, the **British** parliament, the **Russian** leader).

PRACTISE **Spelling 6**, page 36; 'Additional word list'

APPLY Independent writing

ASSESS Dictation: **I travelled all over Europe: France, Portugal, Spain, Russia and Greece.**

Spelling 6   page 37

FOCUS Using a dictionary

TEACH ▶ Ask pupils to explain how they would use a dictionary to help them spell words. ▶ Discuss problems that might arise with finding a word in a dictionary (for example, if someone had misspelt **chemistry** as **kemistry**). ▶ Establish that it is necessary to have some idea of how a word is spelt in order to find it in a dictionary (for example, knowing the first few letters or knowing possible alternative spelling of phonemes to try if the first fails to produce the word). ▶ Ask pupils to locate **chemistry** in their dictionary.

PRACTISE **Spelling 6**, page 37; 'Spelling log' (to record words once found in a dictionary)

APPLY Independent writing

ASSESS Dictation: **The sergeant was trying to manoeuvre the large umbrella through the doorway.**

Spelling 6   page 38

FOCUS Revision 3

TEACH ▶ Recap the different types of spelling strategy (for example, using sounds, word structure, related words). Explain that some words require a mixture of strategies to spell them. ▶ Show examples of spelling errors (for example, **terminul**, **allumineum**). Identify the error; clarify strategies that have been used (for example, sound) and strategies needed to correct the error (for example, links to knowledge of endings). ▶ Establish that good spellers use a mixture of strategies. ▶ Encourage pupils to consider which spelling strategies they use most and which they need to develop.

PRACTISE **Spelling 6**, page 38; 'Words to practise: Spelling practice ladders'

APPLY Respond to marking; proof reading; set personal targets

ASSESS Through independent writing

Spelling 6   page 39

FOCUS Personal spelling list

TEACH ▶ Help pupils compile their own list of ten words to learn and remember. Encourage them to choose words that they frequently get wrong or ones that will be useful in their own writing, either in English or another subject area. ▶ Show them how to categorise errors they are making (for example, wrong spelling choice for the sound, misspelling/missing an unstressed vowel) and encourage them to select strategies to help them remember the correct spelling.

PRACTISE **Spelling 6**, page 39; 'Words to practise: My topic words'

APPLY Set mini-target; independent writing

ASSESS Pupils work in pairs to compose dictation sentences to test each other on chosen words.